WOMEN AND LITERACY

WOMEN AND WORLD DEVELOPMENT SERIES

This series has been developed by the **Joint UN/NGO Group on Women and Development** and makes available the most recent information, debate and action being taken on world development issues, and the impact on women. Each volume is fully illustrated and attractively presented. Each outlines its particular subject, as well as including an introduction to resources and guidance on how to use the books in workshops and seminars. The aim of each title is to bring women's concerns more directly and effectively into the development process, and to achieve an improvement in women's status in our rapidly changing world.

The Group was established in 1980 to organize the production and distribution of Joint UN/NGO development education materials. It was the first time that United Nations agencies and non-governmental organizations had collaborated in this way, and the Group remains a unique example of co-operation between international and non-governmental institutions. Membership of the Group is open to all interested organizations.

SERIES TITLES – in order of scheduled publication

● **WOMEN AND THE WORLD ECONOMIC CRISIS** PREPARED BY JEANNE VICKERS

● **WOMEN AND DISABILITY** PREPARED BY ESTHER R. BOYLAN

● **WOMEN AND HEALTH** PREPARED BY PATRICIA SMYKE

● **WOMEN AND THE ENVIRONMENT** PREPARED BY ANNABEL RODDA

● **REFUGEE WOMEN** PREPARED BY SUSAN FORBES MARTIN

● **WOMEN AND LITERACY** PREPARED BY MARCELA BALLARA

● **WOMEN AND THE FAMILY** PREPARED BY HELEN O'CONNELL

● **WOMEN AT WORK** PREPARED BY CHRISTINE ELSTOB

● **WOMEN AND HUMAN RIGHTS** PREPARED BY KATARINA TOMASEVŠKI

● **WOMEN AND PARTICIPATION**

For full details, as well as order forms, please write to:
ZED BOOKS LTD, 57 CALEDONIAN ROAD, LONDON N1 9BU, U.K. and 165 First Avenue, Atlantic Highlands, New Jersey 07716, U.S.A.

WOMEN AND LITERACY

PREPARED BY MARCELA BALLARA

Zed Books Ltd · London & New Jersey

Women and Literacy was first published by Zed Books Ltd,
57 Caledonian Road, London N1 9BU, United Kingdom and 165 First Avenue,
Atlantic Highlands, New Jersey 07716, United States of America, in 1992.

Cover and book design by Lee Robinson
Cover photo: Osman Akuze, UNEDBAS (UNESCO)
Typeset by Goodfellow & Egan, Cambridge
Printed and bound in the United Kingdom at The Bath Press, Avon

British Library Cataloguing in Publication Data

A catalogue record for this book is available from the British Library

ISBN 1 85649 980 9 hb
ISBN 1 85649 981 7 pb

Library of Congress Cataloging-in-Publication Data

A catalog record for this book is available from the US Library of Congress

CONTENTS

ACKNOWLEDGEMENTS

The Joint UN-NGO Group on Women and Development wishes to acknowledge and thank the following organizations for their participation in the preparation of this book:

OVERALL COORDINATION AND FINANCIAL CONTRIBUTION:

- The International Literacy Year Secretariat of the United Nations Educational, Scientific and Cultural Organization (UNESCO)

The content of this book has been approved by the Joint UN-NGO Group on Women and Development, which wishes to thank all those United Nations specialized agencies, non-governmental organizations and individuals who generously contributed articles and information towards the preparation of this book. References and credits are to be found wherever these were used. The following organizations have made a special contribution through their participation in the editorial panel formed for this publication:

- Catholic International Education Office
- Friends World Committee for Consultation (Quakers)
- International Abolitionist Federation
- International Alliance of Women
- International Association of Charities of Saint Vincent de Paul
- International Catholic Girls' Society
- International Federation for Home Economics
- International Federation of University Women
- International Reading Association
- Société Biblique Suisse
- Soroptimist International
- United Nations Children's Fund (UNICEF)
- Women's International Democratic Federation
- World Association of Girl Guides and Girl Scouts
- World Confederation of Organizations of the Teaching Profession
- World Federation of Trade Unions
- World Movement of Mothers
- World Union of Catholic Women's Organizations
- Zonta International

Overall coordination and management of the Joint UN-NGO Group on Women and Development is provided by the **United Nations Non-Governmental Liaison Service (NGLS)**, an inter-agency unit which fosters dialogue and co-operation between the UN system and the NGO community on development policy and North-South relations.

PREFACE

Education is a powerful agent of progress. Literacy is the most basic and necessary of learning skills.

WOMEN'S LITERACY is the challenge of the decade. It is essential to development, which is impossible without the participation of women. But their involvement depends to a very large extent upon their education.

Today, all development agencies agree on the importance of educating women in order to promote and maintain family education, health, nutrition and general well-being. In all parts of the world, agency programmes dealing with the environment, with health education, with income-generating schemes and so on rely upon women's education to ensure their success.

This book is a contribution towards that success. It shows in practical ways how to go about making women literate, and gives examples of programmes from all over the world. It also constitutes a unique example of co-operation between different international non-governmental organizations (NGOs) and United Nations agencies concerned with the status of women.

Even before *Women and Literacy* appeared in print there was an avalanche of requests from the most diverse groups of women and men concerned with the subject, an indication of how desperately information is needed on this particular theme.

It is hoped that this 'encyclopaedia on literacy for women' will be followed by many other publications on the subject, and that research in this new field will flourish in the coming decade.

It is also hoped that *Women and Literacy* will be a source of inspiration for literacy workers in industrialized as well as developing countries. For it has become ever more clear that a fully-literate world can only be attained through greater attention to women's literacy.

MARIA LUISA JAUREGUI DE GAINZA,
Literacy Specialist with UNESCO.

Literacy programme in the Cape Verde Islands

INTRODUCTION:
LITERACY – THE KEY
TO DEVELOPMENT

IN RECENT YEARS much has been written on the importance of women's participation in the development process. Studies have pointed out the negative effects on women and young girls of the economic crisis and the stabilization and structural adjustment programmes (SAPs) implemented in the 1980s in many developing countries.

Over the last few decades a number of actions have been taken to promote the equality of women in society. In 1967 the General Assembly of the United Nations adopted the Declaration on the Elimination of Discrimination against Women, as part of the Universal Declaration of Human Rights. In 1980 this measure was strengthened when the Assembly proclaimed the Convention on the Elimination of All Forms of Discrimination against Women.

Between 1975 and 1985 the United Nations adopted an Action Plan for the newly designated Decade for Women. Equality, development and peace were declared the basic principles for the implementation of women's programmes, with special reference to equality of opportunity in education. But in spite of all the efforts made, the Decade only partially achieved its aims.

THE NAIROBI CONFERENCE ☐ The results were thoroughly debated at an important meeting held in Nairobi in 1985 known as the World Conference to Review and Appraise the Achievements of the United Nations Decade for Women: Equality, Development and Peace. Since that Conference, which produced the Nairobi Forward-Looking Strategies for the Advancement of Women, new measures have been proposed to overcome the obstacles encountered during the UN Decade for Women, the aim being to ensure that they are implemented before the year 2000.

While progress towards ensuring gender equality has been achieved in some countries, practical measures have yet to be taken. In many instances women's position is still far from satisfactory. Their lower status in both industrialized and developing countries is rooted in economic inequalities, discrimination with regard to access to power, society's reluctance to change attitudes and sexually discriminatory practices, customs and habits that negatively affect the education of women and girls, and ignorance of legal rights due to the influence of cultural models.

Within this context the Nairobi Conference highlighted three sub-themes – employment, health and education – as milestones in enhancing equality, development and peace, education being seen as the basis for the promotion and improvement of women's status and a tool to support their role as equal partners in society.

THE UNESCO PROGRAMME ☐ Already, at the beginning of the 1980s, Unesco had begun to implement plans and strategies in co-operation with Member States and international non-governmental organizations (NGOs) in the field of women's education. A special programme, Equal Opportunities in Education for Women and Girls, was launched with the aim of reducing gender disparities among the various social programme groups, its main objectives being promotion of the equality of women and increasing their participation in development in the interests of justice and peace.[1] Educational programmes for women are affected simultaneously by several multifaceted factors, but regardless of methods or specific educational goals, all such programmes work towards improving women's condition and position in society.

Proposals within the Equal Opportunities programme suggest that literacy projects, which include knowledge in such different fields as health, agriculture, employment, environment and others, can play an important role in promoting development and well-being, and in improving women's quality of life. Nevertheless, a consensus exists today that these goals are not ends in themselves; they can make a significant contribution if they are linked to development strategies and if, at the same time, radical changes are enacted.

To define literacy activities which can support and raise the status of women and girls, one must distinguish between two fundamental and linked aspects of the situation: the condition and position of women. According to one writer, the condition of women means 'the material state in which women find themselves: their poverty, their lack of education and training, their excessive work burdens, their lack of access to modern technology, improved tools, work-related skills, etc.' Position of women refers to 'their social and economic standing relative to men'.[2]

Taking these aspects into account, short- and long-term needs can be defined which, in turn, will provide the elements needed to define policies and strategies that can contribute to improving women's situation.

THE GENDER QUESTION □ Although existing literature notes advances in the general conditions of life for men and women over the last two decades, it is also evident that women have been less favoured. For them, the issue of their status is the main preoccupation, and views reflect three main tendencies.

The first points to a worsening of the situation of women as a result of developing countries' incorporation into the market economy. The marginalization of women arises from their non-integration into the new forms of political organization created by a male-oriented economy that relies on Western stereotypes.

The second rejects the homogeneous category of 'women', focusing instead on the concept of 'gender', arguing that while the term 'women' implies a homogeneous group, the term 'gender' disaggregates women's roles and responsibilities into socio-economic class, agro-ecological environment, and farming system, culture and ethnic group and – within each of these categories – by age, marital status and stage in the household cycle.[3] This distinction suggests that there has to be a clear definition of the target group at which literacy and post-literacy programmes are to be aimed. In turn, a preliminary study on women's situation in a particular society will be necessary in order to meet their basic learning needs, support self-confidence and raise their status.

Women's practical gender needs derive from the necessity to fulfil the roles allocated to them by the traditional sexual division of labour: care and education of children, maintenance of the household, care of the elderly and the infirm, servicing of husband and his relevant kin, maintenance of the network of familial ties, servicing of the community (which in turn enables women to carry out their family based tasks).[4]

The third view can be described as being of a feminist nature: it assumes that women share common experiences of oppression and subordination, basically due to the sexual division of labour which relegates women to the productive and reproductive roles, and to the organization of their sexual life which limits their freedom.

An examination of trends in literacy programmes organized by women reveals several experiments which concentrate mainly on activities that meet practical needs in helping to improve their condition. In other words, they focus on short-term objectives. Thus, it is common to find literacy activities combined with home economics (sewing, embroidery, weaving and cooking) which places more emphasis on their productive and reproductive roles.

WOMEN'S LITERACY, A DEVELOPMENT PRIORITY □

There are many social, economic and cultural reasons which justify special actions to make literacy for women and girls a top priority. Acquisition of knowledge is one of the prerequisites of human development. Literacy and post-literacy activities specifically for women in a single educational process provide for women's participation in sustainable development[5] under equal conditions and with equal benefits; they must be available to all women in order to enhance their individual, economic, political, social and cultural development, and that of the communities in which they live.

In order to achieve this, the United Nations initiated a world movement to promote literacy, and proclaimed 1990 as International Literacy Year, its role being to mobilize and inform the public. UNESCO for its part proposed a 'Plan of Action for the Eradication of Illiteracy by the Year 2000', and organized with other UN agencies a World Conference on Education for All, whose recommendations are to be found in Chapter 4.

This book focuses on the impact of literate women and girls on key areas of development, reviewing the necessary conditions to be fulfilled if a women's literacy programme or project is to succeed. It gives a series of examples of such programmes and projects conceived within the framework of objectives and actions proposed by the Nairobi Conference, by UNESCO and its Member States, and by international NGOs, i.e. having at least one of five major attributes: they have contributed to improving women's status; were concerned with women's and family health; were designed to protect the environment and benefit rural women; were concerned with supporting children's schooling and education; and improved employment opportunities for women. It defines literacy and illiteracy, and outlines UN initiatives to promote out-of-school literacy for women and girls. It is not a theoretical study, but rather a tool for individuals and action groups who wish both to broaden their knowledge and to carry out literacy and post-literacy activities.

The book's objectives are to show the links between various factors affecting gender-specific illiteracy; to develop awareness of the effects of women's and girls' illiteracy on society and upon the development process; to enhance knowledge with regard to how individuals, groups and organizations are reacting in the struggle against women's illiteracy and to improve their status in society; to support organizations in both North and South which wish to work in the areas of literacy, post-literacy and basic education; to increase understanding of the problems faced by illiterate women and girls and their desire for programmes and projects aimed at meeting their specific needs; to provide basic information in order to prepare teaching material to support women's literacy and post-literacy activities; and to encourage individuals and groups to discuss, research and develop solutions for eradicating illiteracy among girls and women, as well as to propose innovative strategies for both North and South.

The improvement of both the position and the condition of women is dependent on structural changes in society. This book proposes options which emphasize both the cultural and ideological aspects of the problem and the need to modify laws and institutions in a market economy.

1. UNESCO (1983) Equality and Education Opportunity for Girls and Women (ED-83/WS/55). Paris.
2. K. Young (ed) (1988) *Women and Economic Development: Local, Regional and National Planning Strategies*. Paris/Oxford, UNESCO/Berg, pp. 1–2
3. United Nations (1989a), Elements of an International Development Strategy for the 1990s: View and Recommendations of the Committee for Development Planning, New York, (ST/ESA/214), p.397.
4. K. Young, *op cit.* 1988, p.6.
5. In the UN context, sustainable development should be understood as the use of renewable resources without violating the ecological system, over-exploiting natural resources or destroying cultures and societies.

FINDING A DEFINITION

Literacy properly understood is not only an initiation in the three Rs but also an apprenticeship in coping with the modern world.

COLIN POWER, UNESCO ASSISTANT
SECRETARY-GENERAL.[1]

BEFORE WE CAN APPROACH THE SUBJECT in any depth we must first understand what is meant by the term 'literacy', particularly as it relates to industrialized and to developing countries. While the meaning of the term may vary according to the required level of literacy and numeracy, the causes and consequences of illiteracy are nevertheless similar, whether for individuals or societies. Literacy is more than knowing the three Rs.

Literacy is the apprenticeship for the knowledge needed to cope with everyday needs, including the individual's relationship with the surrounding world. Hence literacy and post-literacy activities make up a single education process, and literacy policies and strategies must necessarily include both in one action.

'Functional illiteracy', a term used in industrialized countries to refer to those who possess basic literacy and numeracy skills which are not sufficient for proper functioning – i.e. remaining unable to read or write or to make sense of written material – continues to have negative effects at individual, familial and societal levels and is a formidable obstacle to sustainable development.

THE NEGATIVE EFFECTS OF ILLITERACY
☐ These are most acute in developing countries where poverty is generally closely associated with the high illiteracy rate in these countries. Ninety-five per cent of the illiterates of the world are concentrated in developing countries, especially in South-East Asia and sub-Saharan Africa.

Women are the most affected: one-third are illiterate, compared with one-fifth of men. Among the reasons for this are the economic crisis and adjustment policies implemented during the 1980s, which led governments to make substantial cuts in health and education spending. These measures have also had negative economic results for women, resulting in what is known as the 'feminization of poverty'.[2]

Less investment in the education sector and the feminization of poverty are reflected in fewer schooling opportunities for young women and girls. Socio-cultural factors have aggravated educational deprivation. Extremely poor families tend, when possible, to educate their sons, who are seen as potential providers of greater future income. Young women and girls are therefore relegated to domestic and agricultural tasks. Unequal access to schooling and high drop-out rates are important causes of illiteracy among girls and young women, and their number will increase the already large number of illiterate women if urgent measures are not implemented to solve this problem.

In a literate society, it is necessary to know how to read, write and calculate. Those who lack this knowledge find their options limited and their way of life more difficult. Acquiring literacy allows silent women to find a language and express their needs, interest, and concerns. Literacy activities for and with women motivate the organization of women's groups to support collective demands and to seek active participation in development and a better position in society. In this sense, literacy for women is empowering.

LITERACY PROGRAMMES FOR WOMEN
☐ Literacy activities can provide a context and a reason for gathering togeth-

THE GOVERNMENT'S EXTERNAL DEBT HAS RISEN TO $38,000,000. HAVING PROMISED TO IMPOSE NEW AUSTERITY MEASURES, THE GOVERNMENT WILL BE ANNOUNCING A NEW CURRENCY DEVALUATION TOMORROW!!

a. barreto
a. batista
1988

AND IN THE OFFICE...

DID YOU HEAR THE NEWS ABOUT THE DEVALUATION

WHAT'S THAT? ARE PRICES RISING AGAIN?

PROBABLY, BECAUSE DEVALUATION OCCURS WHEN OUR MONEY LOSES VALUE AGAINST GOLD & THE U.S. $.

AND WHAT DOES THIS HAVE TO DO WITH OUR EXTERNAL DEBT?

DEBT? WHAT DEBT? I DON'T OWE ANYBODY ANYTHING! I ALWAYS PAY MY BILLS

YOU DO RITA, BUT OUR GOVERNMENT OWES LOTS OF MONEY TO THE IMF AND OTHER FINANCING AGENCIES LIKE THE WORLD BANK AND CITIBANK

THE DEBT ORIGINATED WITH LOANS TAKEN OUT YEARS AGO BY THIRD WORLD GOVERNMENTS SO THAT THEY COULD INVEST IN LARGE-SCALE PROJECTS

AH! BUT THAT'S THE GOVERNMENT'S DEBT, NOT OURS.

YES, BUT THE DEBT AFFECTS ALL OF US DIRECTLY

HOW?

DEVALUATION AND THE OTHER AUSTERITY MEASURES ARE A RESULT OF THE DEBT. OUR COUNTRIES DON'T HAVE ENOUGH MONEY, BECAUSE THEY ARE PAYING OFF THEIR LOANS, SO THE GOVERNMENT HAS TO REDUCE PUBLIC SERVICES...

...SUCH AS HOUSING, HEALTH, EDUCATION & EMPLOYMENT PROGRAMMES, AFFECTING WOMEN THE MOST BECAUSE THEY ARE THE POOREST...

GULP!

REALLY!

OFFICE

WHAT'S GOING ON HERE? GET TO WORK! THE DEVALUATION HAS NOTHING TO DO WITH YOU!

er to discuss problems and seek solutions. Women often find it easier to talk freely and share their experiences when no men are present. For many women, in both South and North, literacy programmes are an important social experience which also provide support for dealing with their personal concerns. They help to break the isolation deriving from their home environment or employment. Relations developed in such groups support women in learning how to ask for help when needed. In the long run, participating women gain more self-confidence and self-esteem.

Such activities also provide an alternative for those who find it difficult to engage in other courses, either because cultural or religious patterns hamper their participation in mixed groups or because lack of time makes it difficult for them to cope with a regular schedule. Learning to read, write and calculate makes women self-reliant; able to make decisions concerning their own lives, take better care of themselves and their family, protect the environment and natural resources, support their children's education and get better jobs.

Nonetheless, women in developing countries do not always regard literacy as an immediate and important need. Their condition of oppression and poverty is often an obstacle to understanding that being literate could help them to achieve a higher status in their community. In such cases, activities should first be organized to solve their survival needs. Later, at the participants' request, a literacy course can be launched to enhance their standing in the community.

---

1. Colin Power, UNESCO's Assistant Director-General for Education, International Literacy Year 1990. in *ILY: A Year of Opportunity.*

2. For more information on the subject see Jeanne Vickers (1991) *Women and World Development.* Zed Books. London.

② THE GLOBAL CONTEXT

The statistics highlight the *de facto* discrimination against women in education. Various forms of patriarchal and economic oppression subordinate women according to the history and culture of each country and region... Lack of access to school accounts for most adult illiteracy. The traditional sex division of roles in the family and the society exclude most girls from learning literacy through schooling.¹

DESPITE ALL EFFORTS, in 1990 there were 948 million illiterates in the world – a figure which has not changed substantially since 1985. If efforts to deal with the problem are not intensified, projections for the year 2000 indicate at best only a very slight decrease (see Table 2.1).

Rapid population growth, poverty and certain political and economic mechanisms in society, all linked to incomplete coverage of primary education for school-age children, are at the root of the constant increase in the absolute numbers of illiterates in the world.

It is a fact that more women then men are illiterate, and there are many reasons for this. In most societies women have lower status than men. From childhood on they have less access to education, and sometimes to food and health care. As adults, not only do they frequently receive less education, but work longer hours, have lower incomes and little or no access to ownership of property.

Discrimination against females starts early. In many developing countries more girls than boys die between the ages of one and four, a stark contrast with the industrialized countries, where deaths of boys are more than 20 per cent higher than those of girls.²

In all the developing countries, the percentage of literate women is lower than that of literate men. Socio-cultural factors and discrimination against women are the basis of this situation. Such discrimination can take different forms, as the following example shows.

Girls receive less health care and food than boys. A study in Bangladesh showed that 14 per cent of girls, as against 5 per cent of boys, are malnourished. Women typically work about 25 per cent more hours than men, but their total remuneration is less.³ Women are usually concentrated either in the rural areas or in the informal sector of urban areas, where pay levels tend to be lower than in the formal sector of the economy. Gender-specific inequalities are reinforced by unequal access to education. Girls often are simply not sent to school, or drop out earlier, thereby increasing the level of illiteracy among women.

This chapter examines gender-specific discrimination and how it is reflected in the educational statistics, with particular reference to developing countries, and then goes on to assess the social benefit to be gained from literacy for women in terms of sustainable development. It will stress the fact that, despite the motivation manifested by numerous women wishing to participate in literacy programmes, many obstacles often prevent their full participation.

THE LITERACY GAP ☐ According to UNESCO, in 1990 there were 917 million adult illiterates in developing countries (97 per cent of the world's illiterate population), and a relatively insignificant number, 32 million (3 per cent) in the 'developed' or industrialized countries, as can be seen in Table 2.1.

Table 2.1 TOTAL AND ILLITERATE POPULATION AGED 15 YEARS AND OVER (IN MILLIONS)

	TOTAL POPULATION AGED 15 YEARS AND OVER				ILLITERATES			
	1970	1985	1990	2000	1970	1985	1990	2000
WORLD	2 311.5	3 226.2	3 580.7	4 293.6	890.1	949.5	948.1	935.4
DEVELOPING COUNTRIES	1 540.7	2 307.6	2 626.1	3 272.7	842.3	907.2	916.6	919.7
Sub-Saharan Africa	148.6	226.1	263.4	364.4	115.0	133.9	138.8	146.8
Arab States	67.6	107.5	125.4	172.7	49.7	58.6	61.1	65.6
Latin America/Caribbean	164.0	252.1	286.9	362.7	43.0	44.6	43.9	41.7
Eastern Asia	692.5	1 036.3	1 171.3	1 375.1	324.1	295.3	278.8	236.5
Southern Asia	440.0	648.4	738.6	952.2	302.3	374.8	398.1	437.1
Least developed countries	135.2	212.3	245.4	333.4	104.8	138.4	148.2	170.1
DEVELOPED COUNTRIES	770.8	918.6	954.6	1 020.9	47.8	42.3	31.5	15.7
CLASSIFICATION BY CONTINENTS								
AFRICA	200.3	305.2	354.3	485.5	152.6	171.8	177.5	186.4
AMERICA	326.0	459.4	503.6	598.1	52.8	54.7	50.4	42.5
ASIA	1 253.9	1 846.8	2 088.7	2 538.3	652.0	694.4	699.7	695.5
EUROPE AND USSR	518.1	597.0	614.6	649.3	31.1	26.9	19.1	9.7
OCEANIA	13.1	17.8	19.4	22.3	1.5	1.7	1.4	1.2

Source: Unesco Compendium of Statistics on Illiteracy – 1990 Edition (Statistical Reports and Studies), p.5

In 1990, Eastern and Southern Asia accounted for 71 per cent of the world's total illiterate, sub-Saharan Africa for 15 per cent, the Arab States for 6 per cent and Latin America and the Caribbean for less than 5 per cent. In both Southern Asia and the Arab states one adult out of two is illiterate.

It should be emphasized that several practical difficulties exist in collecting and processing illiteracy statistics, both at global and regional levels; this should be kept in mind when such data are interpreted. Nevertheless, the statistics are indicative of the general trends and show the scale of efforts required in the struggle against illiteracy, either by region or sub-region.

GENDER DISPARITIES ☐ That the large concentration of illiterates is found among women is extensively documented.

Invariably women represent the largest share of the illiterate population and will continue to do so

states a UNESCO study that presents projections for 1990 as illustrated in Table 2.2.

While almost half – 45 per cent – of the female population of developing countries is illiterate, the figure in the least developed countries rises to 79 per cent of adult women. In Africa 64 per cent of women cannot read and write. Discrimination against women's education in the least developed countries is evident; in the mid-1980s fewer than half the school-age girls were enrolled in primary school, less than 10 per cent in secondary education, and less than 1 per cent at the post-secondary level.

In absolute numbers, the vast majority of women who cannot read and write is concentrated in Asia; illiterate women in this region alone account for over 77 per cent of the world total.[5] Clearly, if gender disparities regarding illiteracy are to be reduced, major efforts must be made in Asia and Africa.[14]

Table 2.2 DEVELOPING COUNTRIES ILLITERACY RATES BY SEX (%) 1990

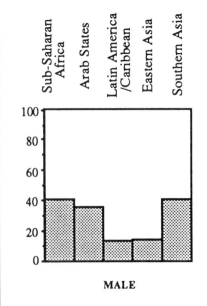

MALE

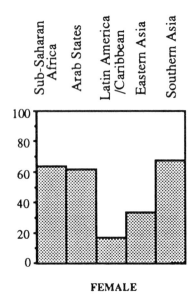

FEMALE

Source: UNESCO, 1989.

URBAN/RURAL DISPARITIES ☐ The data presented in Table 2.3 are particularly interesting because they were collected in the 1979-82 period about a population whose age ranged from 15 to 25 years old. These people are now between 25 and 35 years old; they are actively involved in their reproductive and productive roles, and are probably permanently illiterate.

The great difference between women and men in rural/urban sectors, and between women involved in both sectors, is illustrated. The rate of illiterate women in the rural sector is higher than that of urban women, an important factor to be considered when educational activities are planned for the rural sector.[6]

THE AGE FACTOR ☐ UNESCO figures for 1990 in developing countries indicate there were 368 million children between the ages of 16 and 17 who did not attend school. Some 125 million children

between 6 and 11 years were not enrolled in school in 1990. In 16 developing countries primary school enrolment for girls is two-thirds lower than for boys. In 17 countries the secondary school enrolment rate for girls is half that for boys.[7]

These children will be adult illiterates by the start of the twenty-first century if urgent steps are not taken now to reverse falling educational levels, stagnation of school enrolment and qualitative decline.

ILLITERACY IN INDUSTRIALIZED COUNTRIES ☐ The world economic crisis that began in the 1970s exacerbated the problem of the functional illiterate in industrialized countries. UNESCO has defined a functional illiterate as:

a person who cannot engage in all those activities in which literacy is required for effective functioning of his group and community and also for enabling him to continue to use reading, writing and calculation for his own and the community's development.

Table 2.3 ILLITERACY RATE FOR THE 15–19 AGE GROUP IN URBAN AND RURAL AREAS (%)

REGION		FEMALE ILLITERACY		MALE ILLITERACY	
		URBAN	RURAL	URBAN	RURAL
Africa	Benin	59.0	92.1	31.4	68.3
	Togo	34.3	66.4	9.2	28.7
	United Republic of Tanzania	21.2	43.5	7.1	18.4
Latin America	Brazil	7.6	29.4	9.4	37.3
	Ecuador	2.4	10.6	1.6	7.8
Asia	Afghanistan	56.4	93.8	31.4	55.7
	Bangladesh	52.1	74.6	42.1	60.9
	China	3.2	16.6	1.4	4.7
	India	29.2	66.3	17.9	39.6
	Indonesia	7.0	19.6	3.3	12.2
	Nepal	46.5	85.2	27.0	53.8
	Pakistan	45.9	86.9	36.7	63.8
	Philippines	2.9	10.1	3.2	12.0
	Sri Lanka	5.6	11.2	4.8	10.6

Source: UNESCO, Compendium of Statistics on Illiteracy (Paris, 1988).

Diagram 2.1 EDUCATION: THE HIGHER THE EDUCATION THE GREATER THE SEX GAP

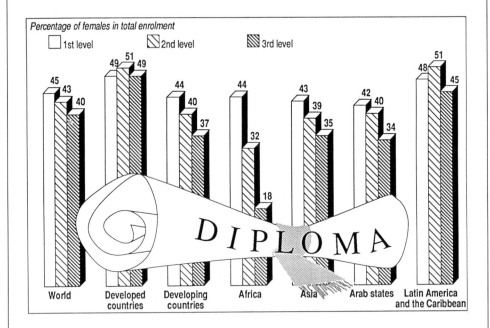

Source : Unesco Office of Statistics

Girls and women are well behind men and boys in terms of education, as is clearly shown in the above graph. The figures are based on the three globally recognized levels of education - primary, secondary and tertiary.

The percentage of female students only cracks the 50 per cent mark in two cases - in secondary education in the developed countries and in the region of Latin America and the Caribbean. The figures for these two zones show almost a parity between male and female students, and reflects the differences between the male and female populations. Tertiary education in Latin America and the Caribbean is the only area where this parity drops off.

However, everywhere else girls and women are clearly worse off, and the higher the level of education the greater the disparity. The situation for females in the Arab States and Asia is comparable, with only one student in three being a woman. The gap is most marked in Africa where less than one primary or secondary student in three, and less than one tertiary student in five is female.

Source: UNESCO Sources No.5, June 1989

These people lead a normal life but are incapable of coping with routine literacy tasks. This is not due to a lack of knowledge, but does indicate the need for an increase in education to enable participation in the social, political and economic environment, as well as fuller integration into the labour force where technical progress is steadily increasing.[8]

As functional illiteracy is a relatively recent and infrequent phenomenon in the industrialized countries (except in the United States), functional illiterates often feel a sense of personal failure and shame; some tend to withdraw from society, whereas in countries where illiteracy is a generalized phenomenon it is regarded neither as a stigma nor as a reason for social exclusion.

Problems in determining the exact number of functional illiterates have been aggravated by the fact that individuals find it difficult to acknowledge that they fall into this category. The most reliable data have been provided by military or prison services, but this is not sufficient. A technical meeting of specialists from 23 countries of the European region, organized by UNESCO in Hamburg, estimated that ten per cent of the population of industrialized countries cannot read or write adequately. They also noted that:

because of the wide range of situations covered by illiteracy, the many different operative criteria in the various countries and the difficulty of identifying the functionally illiterate, no precise statistical data are as yet available.⁹

Nevertheless, several countries have begun to investigate this situation. The United States Department of Education has acknowledged that 20 per cent of Americans aged over 17, or 27 million people, are functionally illiterate. An additional 45 million are barely competent in the basic literacy skills. Several studies have shown that those having difficulties in reading and writing include the unemployed (75 per cent), young delinquents (85 per cent), prisoners (60 per cent) and ethnic minorities (40 per cent).

THE EFFECT ON WOMEN □ The National Coalition for Women and Girls in Education (USA) links the prevalence of functional illiteracy to teenage pregnancies, crime, chronic unemployment and long-term dependence on social welfare. Women, and young women in particular, are affected socio-economically;

Ethiopian refugees in Sudan

PHOTO: UNHCR/S. ERRINGTON

those below the poverty line and the average educational level are 5.5 times more likely to be teenage mothers.

Some 65 per cent of female heads of households living in poverty have not completed secondary level education, compared with 44 per cent of males in a similar situation. Some 40 per cent of single mothers have completed less than eight years of schooling.

An increasing number of women support their families. If their literacy level continues to be low, it is likely that the illiteracy cycle will remain self-perpetuating. Children of illiterate parents are disadvantaged compared with their peers, and will probably follow the pattern set by their parents.

In Canada, the *Southam Literacy Report*[10] revealed that there were five million functional illiterates in that country. Moreover, illiteracy among men is higher (53.3 per cent) than it is for women (46.5 per cent) and more common among adults over the age of 55. Some eight per cent of the population over 15 is fundamentally illiterate. Data suggest that the annual increase in

illiteracy will be around 30,000 over the next few years.

Functional illiteracy affects women and young girls differently, based on the particular characteristics of each country. However, this phenomenon is undeniably concentrated in the poorest sections of a community, and among ethnic minorities and the handicapped. The implications of this are in turn linked with social status, economic possibilities, access to employment and participation in civic and cultural life.[11]

The data presented in this chapter highlight the fact that efforts to increase women's literacy rates have not produced the expected results. This is undoubtedly one of the most difficult problems to be faced during the present decade. Sustainable development cannot be attained either in the short- or long-term if a population is unable to read, write and calculate. Without these skills, it will be difficult for women to understand, improve and change their social and physical environment.

1. A. Lind and H. Johnston (1986) *Adult Literacy in the Third World: A Review of Objectives and Strategies*, Stockholm, Institute of International Education, University of Stockholm/Swedish International Development Agency.
2. United Nations Development Programme (UNDP), *Human Development Report 1990*, New York/Oxford University Press, p.31.
3. Ibid., p.32.
4. United Nations, 1990.
5. Data Highlights No.6, Female Adult Illiteracy, 1989.
6. Ibid.
7. UNDP, 1990.
8. J.W. Ryan (1980) 'Linguistic Factors in Adult Literacy', *Literacy Review*, Tehran pp.57–87.
9. Workshop of Specialists in Europe on Prevention of Functional Illiteracy and Integration of Youth into the World of Work, Hamburg, 1986.
10. Southam Newspaper Group (1987), 'Broken Words: Why Five Million Canadians are Illiterate' in *The Southam Literary Report*, Toronto.
11. J.W. Ryan, 1980.

THE LEGACY OF FEMALE ILLITERACY

Why are so many women illiterate? Whatever the potential advantages literacy may hold for women in developing countries it continues to be an abstract notion.

IN SITUATIONS OF EXTREME POVERTY it may well be necessary to resolve such problems as food shortages, poor health care, housing, employment and agricultural production before any successful literacy action can be undertaken.[1] In addition, many women living in semi-literate cultures do not feel any social pressure to acquire literacy and numeracy skills, unlike in industrialized countries where the social pressure is strong.[2]

OBSTACLES TO LITERACY □ Even when the motivation is there, formidable obstacles remain. Foremost among them is probably lack of time. The traditional or new roles that women fill rarely leave them enough free time to devote to full-time or even part-time educational activities. Fatigue, frequent or early pregnancies, caring for children and families, agricultural and cultural activities, and formal or informal employment, are among the many reasons for lack of time. This heavy workload is reflected in the high rate of absenteeism and drop-out of women from literacy activities. The same reasons apply to girls' schooling.

Organizational problems – male instructors, mixed gender classes, considerable distances between home and the education centre, lack of transport, evening courses and cultural clashes between instructors and participants – are also constraints to women's full participation in educational activities.

Then again, there is the problem of cultural patterns and customs. Many parents believe that it is not worthwhile to invest in girls' education; instead they invest time and money to educate their sons, who will provide support for them when adult. Daughters are seen as additional sources of household labour who, once married, will become part of the (re)productive labour force of another household. Discrimination against women in the labour market, and in salaries, reinforces parents' negative attitudes towards educating girls.

Husbands, fathers and men in general have such attitudes towards women's education, especially when it results in the possibility of learning new skills which give women a new role in the family. Better earning prospects tend to give women more independence and change their economic status in the family, and this may give rise to family tensions, particularly if women's earnings are controlled by the husband.[3]

Some religious traditions may restrict women's activities to domestic tasks, stressing their role as mothers, which limits their access to education. Lack of self-confidence, timidity, submissiveness to male authority, as well as isolation and age differences between participants, are also limiting factors for women's participation in education. The main reason, however, is the poverty of most illiterate women, which oppresses them in their everyday lives and prevents them from taking an active part in educational activities.

BECOMING LITERATE: THE QUESTION OF MOTIVATION □ Whenever literacy programmes or projects are carried out in

High-density population concentration in Hongkong

developing countries, there is a high level of female participation. Several studies have indicated that the reasons behind this are the changing social roles of women and men. The gradual increase in the number of female heads of households, due in part to the rising number of men leaving home in search of better job opportunities, gives women the responsibility of supporting the family including taking over agricultural production in rural areas, or by entering the informal or formal labour force. Literacy is seen as a tool that will help women carry out these tasks better, once their basic needs have been met. But whether it is a social pressure, or women's new roles, other personal motivations also play an important part when making decisions.

CHILDCARE, EDUCATION AND FAMILY INCOME

These are common reasons given by women, living in industrialized and developing countries in both urban and rural areas, for seeking to become literate. The importance women give to schooling their children for a better future, to providing their children and family with better health care, and the acquisition of income-generating skills, motivate them to take a more active role in literacy activities.

COMMUNICATING WITH THE LITERATE COMMUNITY

It is not sufficient to be able to sign documents; women must also fill in forms, contracts and cheques, keep accounts, write letters and read those received from family members who have emigrated, send cheques, receive money, send telegrams, and read recipes and agricultural instructions. In short, women use literacy and numeracy skills for everything that can provide them with greater autonomy in everyday life.

RELIGIOUS REASONS

Many indigenous groups associate learning to read and write with Christianity, reading the holy scriptures and hymns in church. Some studies have found that religious reasons can play an important role in motivating adults to acquire literacy skills.[4]

SOCIAL CHANGE In countries undergoing revolutionary changes that include widespread political mobilization in support of literacy, women see this as a way to become actors in the process of change their country is experiencing. Examples are to be found in Cuba, Mozambique, Nicaragua and Tanzania.

Even where these and other motivating factors exist, the obstacles already discussed in this chapter often prevent women benefiting from literacy and, in the case of school-age girls, from enrolling in primary eduation, a crucially important stage in preventing girls from becoming future illiterates.

WOMEN'S ROLE IN DEVELOPMENT A number of studies have demonstrated the effect of women's literacy and education in both social and economic development. Women's literacy enables a better use of family planning and results in a fall in birth rate. While this relationship is not always constant, the results of the study carried out by the Demographic Health Survey (DHS) in 1990 in 28 countries in Africa, Latin America and the Caribbean, Asia and the Arab states, noted that the tendency for smaller families increased with the educational level of women. The average number of children fell to less than four among women with secondary education. Family planning methods are more widely used in countries such as Botswana, Kenya and Zimbabwe, where over 70 per cent of women have some education.

Women's education plays an important role in child care, especially in relation to infant mortality levels. A study carried out by the Research Triangle Institute (1990) in 80 developing countries indicated that an increase of 70 per cent in girls' enrolment in primary schools, together with a comparable growth in secondary education, would after 20 years result in a decrease in the infant mortality rate of 40 per 1,000 live births. Such primary and secondary education for women would contribute to a continuation of this decrease, over and above other relevant development inputs such as increased *per capita* income, level of urbanization, medical facilities and male school enrolment. *The State of the World Population* (1990) reported that the results of studies carried out in 46 countries indicated that a one per cent increase in women's literacy rate is three times more effective in reducing infant mortality than a one per cent increase in the number of doctors.

As women's level of education rises, the number of malnourished children declines. DHS (March 1990) found that in Guatemala, where only 65 per cent of the women have had some level of education, the percentage of stunted infants aged 3 to 35 months is over 50 per cent, compared with fewer than 10 per cent in Trinidad and Tobago, where women have a higher level of education. While other factors are relevant, the educational levels of women are of paramount importance.

The same study indicated that pre-natal care and medical treatment at childbirth increases with the mother's level of education. It also has a strong bearing on whether or not children received treatment for diarrhea, one of the major causes of mortality among young children. Use of oral rehydration salts also increases with the mother's education.

Women's literacy has a positive effect on school enrolment and attendance. In Mexico, a study carried out by Muñoz Izquierdo[5] established that adults who completed literacy courses had more daughters with some formal education than those who had not finished their studies.

WOMEN IN THE LABOUR FORCE □

The number of women participating in the labour force in the formal sector is directly related to their educational level. The Triangle Research Institute study showed that a 70 per cent increase in primary and secondary education will, after 20 years, lead to a 7.3. per cent increase in women's participation in the labour force. Many researchers have stressed the close association between the level of education and productivity increase in the modern sector of the economy. Nevertheless, the increasing trend towards reducing the number of jobs in the formal sector most directly affects disadvantaged groups such as women.

Women's literacy also increases productivity and self-employment in the informal sector. The trend towards an increase in the number of self-employed women, or of those who work on a sub-contract basis, opens up several possibilities, particularly for those women who are their family's only means of economic support. Examples of successful activities linking literacy with income-earning are found among projects aimed at setting up small enterprises to meet market needs and ensure the continuity of economic activities.

Increased productivity in the agricultural sector is also linked to the educational level of rural women. This is shown by a study on the effects of education on productivity in agriculture in a number of developing countries. This study concluded that four years of primary education (usually considered the minimum level for retaining literacy) increased productivity by 7.4 per cent, with additional benefits in the form of increased modernization of agriculture. Production incentives, marketing facilities, distribution of seeds and fertilizers and rural extension programmes are also important.[6] Literacy helps people acquire necessary knowledge, make better use of natural resources and protect the environment; it facilitates a change in attitudes that can encourage increased productivity.

LITERACY AND SUSTAINABLE DEVELOPMENT □ The term 'sustainable development' refers to humanity's ability to survive by means of the rational use of renewable resources, by refraining from disrupting the ecosystem or over-exploiting natural resources, and by refraining from activities that destroy cultures or societies and instead allow them to reach their potential.

Because women play an important role in the development process, radical measures to increase literacy will enhance their participation in development and at the same time improve their status. Action

must be taken during the 1990s to increase efforts by the international community and by governments to provide women and girls with full access to education.

Women must be educated in terms of their crucial role in society, whether as producers or reproducers: they are mainly responsible for the care and well-being of their families; they play an important role as educators of future generations; they fulfil economic functions, in both urban and rural areas, that are vital for the survival of the family (the significant increase in number of female heads of household is again noteworthy).

As part of an individual's personal development, literacy is a right to which everyone – women as well as men – should have access. Acquiring it enables women to increase their self-confidence, improve their self-esteem, become aware of their civil rights, improve their income-earning capabilities and to play an active

Ugandan refugees, repatriated from Sudan under a voluntary scheme which helps them to re-establish themselves

PHOTO: UNHCR/J.COURTIN

role in family and community decision-making. Literacy is a means for women to participate on equal terms in the process of social development and change, for quantitative and qualitative progress in society: in short, for sustainable development.

While women's literacy promotes sustainable development, and plays a major role in socio-economic change, it must be supported by the necessary structural changes in society.

1. K. Chlebowska (1989), *Un temps pour Apprendre*, Paris, UNESCO/UNICEF. L. Ramdas, (1989) 'Women and Literacy: a quest for justice' in *Prospects Quarterly Review of Education*, UM XIX, No. 4, pp. 519–30, Paris, UNESCO; A. Lind and A. Johnston (1986) *Adults Literacy in the Third World*.
2. Ramdas, 1989; H.P. Gerhard 'Literacy for What?', *Prospects*, Vol. XIX, No. 4, pp. 491-504.
3. Lind and Johnston, 1986.
4. S. Scribner and M. Cole, (1981), *The Psychology of Literacy*, Cambridge Mass., Harvard University Press; Gerhard 1989.
5. Izquierdo, 1985.
6. F. Calledois (1989), Women's Literacy for Development, paper presented at Symposium on Women and Literacy, 8–10 June 1989.

INTERNATIONAL RESPONSES

Efforts to increase literacy rates among girls and women must consequently be pursued and indeed intensified. This is the objective of the activities foreseen under the headings of literacy and post-literacy, where special emphasis will be laid on rural women and on programmes which have a direct bearing on their access to the teaching profession and, more generally, to employment opportunities.[1]

THE ELEMENTS SET OUT ABOVE refer to the discrimination and difficulties facing all women and girls in the educational sector. Thus, if large-scale educational activities and strategies in their favour are not promoted, it is highly unlikely that, in this or future decades, a situation of equality will be achieved. This in turn will limit women's participation in and contribution to the political and economic development of society.

In light of this situation, Unesco proposed in 1985 that the United Nations declare a year for literacy. Education is one of the inalienable rights of every person and has been recognized as such in both the Universal Declaration of Human Rights and the Universal Covenant on Economic, Social and Cultural Rights. Since in many developing countries illiteracy still constitutes a serious obstacle to the process of social and economic development, functional literacy and adequate education programmes assume even greater importance as indispensable elements for social development and progress. Recognizing this, the United Nations Assembly declared 1990 as International Literacy Year.[2]

INTERNATIONAL LITERACY YEAR (ILY) **1990** ☐ Launching a year dedicated to literacy provided a unique opportunity for mobilizing national, regional and international efforts in the struggle to extend literacy to the whole of the world's population. Unesco undertook an awareness campaign in order to focus world public opinion on the need to achieve literacy for all by the year 2000, thereby embarking upon a decade devoted to this end.

Informing the public, mobilizing resources and laying the groundwork for educational activities over the new decade were among the various ILY goals, many of which have borne fruit. For example, at the initiative of the International Council for Adult Education (ICAE), based in Canada, more than 30 non-governmental organizations (NGOs) met in 1987 to set up the International Task Force on Literacy (ITFL) to mobilize and promote actions during ILY and throughout the 1990s.

To reduce illiteracy during the 1990s is not an easy task. The economic crisis of the past decade has profoundly affected efforts made in favour of formal and non-formal education. UNICEF's *State of the World's Children* (1990) points out that in the 1980s there was a significant decrease in public expenditure for education; in the 37 poorest countries such expenditures have fallen by approximately 25 per cent of gross national product (GNP), resulting in fewer children aged from 6 to 11 years enrolled in school. It also states that, sadly, more than two-thirds of those children who never go to school or who drop out at an early stage are girls. As the 1990s begin, a girl born in South-East Asia or in the Middle East has less than one chance in three of completing primary education.[3]

Most of these children will be illiterate for the rest of their lives unless they are given a second chance in formal or non-formal education; investment is therefore needed in both sectors.

The struggle to extend literacy to all is a challenge of such dimensions that it will require multi-sectoral collaboration from international, governmental and non-governmental organizations and national governments. A world movement has therefore been organized to unite all efforts towards the achievement of this goal, with the participation of the United Nations system.

This took the form of international actions carried out in 1990, such as UNESCO's Plan of Action for the Eradication of Illiteracy by the Year 2000, and the World Conference on Education for All: Meeting Basic Learning Needs, which took place in Jomtien, Thailand, in March 1990. Both have complementary proposals for countries and international organizations, using a two-track approach based on parallel measures for children and adults, a programme for the universalization of primary education and another for non-formal adult education, including literacy.

UNESCO'S PLAN OF ACTION This identifies four major objectives upon which UNESCO should focus its efforts: (1) alerting world public opinion; (2) rallying the international community; (3) strengthening the regional literacy projects and programmes; and (4) reinforcing technical cooperation with Member States. Two priorities are proposed: (1) to improve the education of women and girls; and (2) to help countries confronting especially severe problems of illiteracy.[4]

These objectives will be implemented through the regional literacy structures established by governments during the past decade, and with the assistance of UNESCO. These include the Major Project in the Field of Education in Latin America and the Caribbean (1981); the Regional Programme for the Eradication

of Illiteracy in Africa (1984); the Regional Programme for Universal Provision and Renewal of Primary Education and Eradication of Illiteracy in Asia and the Pacific – APPEAL – (1987); and the Regional Programme for the Universalization and Renewal of Primary Education and the Eradication of Illiteracy in the Arab States by the Year 2000 – ARABUPEAL – (1989).

Although these regional structures have their own programmes, objectives and modes of functioning, the plan of action in all of them is based on the two-track approach involving universal primary education and non-formal adult education, including literacy teaching.

THE WORLD CONFERENCE ON EDU-CATION FOR ALL □ From 5 to 9 March 1990 the international community met in Jomtien, Thailand, for the purpose of discussing illiteracy. With the participation of Unesco, the United Nations Children's Fund (UNICEF), the United Nations Development Programme (UNDP), the World Bank, 20 inter-governmental agencies, delegates from 155 governments and 150 non-governmental organizations, the conference adopted the World Declaration on Education for All and endorsed the Framework of Action to Meet Basic Learning Needs, which propose specific educational actions for this decade.

The World Declaration on Education for All states that the fundamental role played by basic education in the development of society is an inalienable right for all, in order to meet basic learning needs. These include: literacy, oral expression, knowledge, skills, values and attitudes, not as ends in themselves but as the first steps towards continuing education. The Declaration asserts that in order to meet these basic learning needs, a wider vision should be adopted that involves improving present resources, institutional structures, curricula and conventional delivery systems.

An appeal is made to all sectors of society to increase and mobilize financial and human resources from public, private and voluntary organizations. The need to strengthen international solidarity in order to implement the Declaration is emphasized, and it suggests that more equitable economic relations and reduced inequalities should be promoted.

The Framework for Action to Meet Basic Learning Needs constitutes guidelines for governments, international organizations, non-governmental organizations and others engaged in the struggle against illiteracy. The meeting suggested that countries might wish to set their own targets for the 1990s in terms of the following proposed dimensions:

1. **Expansion of early childhood care and developmental activities, including family and community interventions, especially for poor, disadvantaged and disabled children;**
2. **Universal access to, and completion of, primary education (or whatever higher level of education is considered as 'basic' by the year 2000);**
3. **Improvement in learning achievement such that an agreed percentage of an appropriate age cohort (for example, 80 per cent of 14-year-olds) attains or surpasses a defined level of necessary learning achievement;**
4. **Reduction of the adult illiteracy rate (the appropriate age group to be determined in each country) to, say, one-half of its 1990 level by the year 2000, with sufficient emphasis on female literacy to reduce significantly the current disparity between male and female illiteracy rates;**
5. **Expansion of provisions of basic education and training in other essential skills required by**

Bolivian refugees in literacy classes; under the Rural Development Programme they play a broader role in their community

PHOTO: UNHCR/ROY WITLIN

youth and adults, with programme effectiveness assessed in terms of behavioural changes and impacts on health, employment and productivity;

6. Increased acquisition by individuals and families of the knowledge, skills and values required for better living and sound and sustainable development, made available through all education channels including the mass media, other forms of modern and traditional communication, and social action, with effectiveness assessed in terms of behavioural change.[5]

THE ROLE OF NON-GOVERNMENTAL ORGANIZATIONS □ Non-governmental

organizations (NGOs) are independent groups with their own priorities and programmes. They are not at the service or disposition of government, multilateral or bilateral agencies.[6] They are thus able to foster a new and innovative vision in education and take responsibility for preparing programmes and projects, including the identification, design, implementation and evaluation of basic education programmes. This independence means that NGOs can support parts or all of programmes initiated by governments, although their role in such collaborative efforts needs to be precisely defined in order to avoid duplication of effort.

NGOs have played an important part in educational actions, both in industrialized and developing countries. Likewise, they can make a valuable contribution to future actions in the struggle against illiteracy. The close ties that NGOs have with communities make them well-placed to identify the population's needs and concerns, and to meet basic learning needs. This in turn puts them in an exceptionally good position to motivate and mobilize the public, as well as to extend their influence to areas of the community that state sectors do not reach.

NGOs can broaden their range of action concerning the education of women and girls in the following ways:

- **Functioning as catalysts for change.** The regional networks of NGOs concerned with adult and women's education can serve as lobbies for international organizations in order to increase women's participation in development programmes. National NGOs can play a similar role with their governments to promote women's equal access to education.

- **Mobilizing public opinion** on the need to integrate women into education, and to recognize the obstacles they now face.

- **Motivating women** to take part in basic education programmes in order to improve their condition and position in society, to increase awareness of their rights and their self-confidence, to enhance their aspirations, to question gender stereotypes and relations of inequality that limit their individual development, and, lastly, to support everything that can help improve the quality of their lives, including participation in and equal access to development.

- **Conducting follow-up of women's progress in basic education** by assessing the impact of education on women and supporting the introduction of measures and programmes that favour women's integration in literacy programmes and education in general.

- **Mobilizing funds and resources** to support educational programmes for women.

- **Making use of the mass media** to disseminate useful information addressed to women.

- **Helping to develop facilities** to reduce the excessive load of women's work and to enable them to take part in education programmes by providing such facilities as day-care centres, activities, incentives and transportation.

- **Providing services,** so that participants may increase their income and enter the informal sector of the economy, such as access to credit and assistance in quality control and marketing.

- **Encouraging the creation of, and women's participation in** co-operative groups, micro-enterprises and groups to defend their rights, as well as any organization that may help them to gain self-confidence and contribute to sustainable development.

Non-governmental organizations can make important contributions to the qualitative and quantitative improvement of basic education for all women and girls, especially through their participatory and integrated approach characterizing their actions.

1. UNESCO, 1990e, para. 427.
2. United Nations Resolution 44/127.
3. As cited in J.P. Grant and P. Adamson (1990) The State of the World's Children, New York, UNICEF p. 48.
4. Unesco, General Conference, twenty-fifth session, Paris, 1989. *Plan of Action to Eradicate Illiteracy by the Year 2000*. Paris, UNESCO, 1989 (25 C/71), 'Summary'.

5. World Conference on Education for All: Meeting Basic Learning Needs, Jomtien, Thailand, 1990, *Framework for Action to Meet Basic Learning Needs* (endorsed by the Conference on 9 March 1990), para. 8. New York, Inter-Agency Commission for the World Conference on Education for All, 1990.
6. B.L. Hall, New Perspectives in Literacy: The Role of Non-governmental Organizations. *Prospects, Quarterly Review of Education*, Vol.XIX, No.4, 1989, pp. 573–8.

TACKLING ILLITERACY: SUCCESSFUL PROJECTS

Literacy activities for women and girls have drawn attention to a number of factors which enhance the probability of obtaining positive results and which should be taken into consideration when such literacy work is planned.

The five main factors in planning literacy programmes are political priorities and community support, the integrated approach, literacy and post-literacy, developmental projects, participation and organizations:

1. **Political priorities and community support** Experience shows that political support, at national as well as local levels, particularly in the area where the project or programme is to be implemented, constitutes the main channel for mobilizing women and girls and enabling them to complete literacy programmes. Political support also helps induce hostile groups to adopt a more sympathetic attitude toward accepting the need for women and girls to enrol in educational programmes or take part in activities of a social, political or economic nature.[1]

National and local support also implies a commitment by the state and the community to actions resulting in the mobilization of the population, and contributes to making necessary sources available. It also helps people to become aware that the rights and roles of women extend far beyond production and reproduction.

India's programme, launched in 1986, for the Promotion of Education of Women and Girls is a good example of the way in which political support can be given at national and local levels. The Pilot Project for Literacy and Civic Education for Women, carried out in co-operation with Unesco, is one of several projects implemented in the Northern region of the country among the Hindi-speaking majority (Chinat, Bakshi-ka-Talab, Lucknow and Uttar Pradesh). After only two years this project resulted in 30,000 trained women. Among these, many obtained employment and became more aware of their civic rights; others took primary school certificate examinations. Many became primary school teachers who now, in turn, promote the enrolment of girls in school.

2. **The integrated approach** It has been found advantageous for women and girls' literacy training activities to be linked to a wider project or programme. In this way, literacy can be combined with efforts in health training, civic education, agriculture, handicrafts, technology, small-scale industry and other fields relevant to women's short- and long-term needs. This knowledge can be acquired through short courses combined with remunerative activities. Women's organizations, such as co-operatives, small-scale enterprises, mothers' centres and so on, could be studied as additional subjects.

Following this integrated approach, various NGOs have implemented literacy programmes and projects for women and girls with the aim of improving their condition and their position in the society. In fact, the success of projects carried out by the Young Women's

Christian Association (YWCA) of India derives from combining literacy and numeracy training with courses in health, employment, social education and education concerning women's legal rights. So as to encourage the participation of women in literacy each programme included, for example, handicrafts, dress-making, soap and detergent production and bookbinding, designed to increase family income.

Recently several other NGOs have undertaken programmes and projects with a similar approach, but their final results have not yet been evaluated. These include the World Association of Girl Guides and Girl Scouts (WAGGGS), with programmes in Sierra Leone, Sri Lanka, Senegal and Zimbabwe; Soroptimist International, active in the Province of Cajamarca, Peru; the Associated Country Women of the World (ACWW) in Kenya, India, Zaire, Pakistan and Ecuador; the International Federation of University Women (IFUW) in Senegal (Natam Department): Wanita Katolik Republik Indonesia (WKRI) in co-operation with the Family Welfare Movements (PKK); Wider Opportunities for Women Inc. (WOW) in the United States; and the Baha'i International Community in India and in Kenya. UNESCO and the United Nations Development Fund for Women (UNIFEM) have also initiated projects using this integrated approach.

3. **Literacy and post-literacy training: one educational process** The third factor is the need to plan programmes and projects that consider both literacy and post-literacy work as one single activity – two stages in the same educational plan – which will enable the newly-literate to retain, develop and put into practice the knowledge acquired to improve their quality of life.[2]

The wide-ranging aspect of literacy and post-literacy training as a combined activity also helps participants more readily to remember what they have learned. The planning of such training is even more important for women in rural areas, who are often limited to using vernacular languages that differ from those used in literacy courses.[3]

Tanzania is one of the countries where literacy and post-literacy programmes have been successful, due especially to the establishment of the 'Universities of Popular Development' which, since their creation, have been providing adult education facilities for the newly literate. This programme has been extended to women and girls in order to prepare them for income-generating activities in their communities. Women who have completed their training and set up co-operatives are given an initial loan of raw material and equipment, as well as a guarantee of ongoing technical assistance.

In other countries attempts have been made to continue post-literacy activities in the framework of lifelong education. In Togo, reading rooms, readers' groups, brochures and other publications and cultural activities are being set up. Yemen, with UNICEF support, has organized courses on health addressed to the newly literate, especially women.

Literacy and post-literacy activities are not limited to the production of written material; they also include practical steps that favour the creation of a literate environment, for example organizing community and income-generating activities and setting up co-operatives, day-care centres and small enterprises.

4. **Development projects and meeting women's needs and concerns** It is essential to link these pro-

grammes to development strategies, both at national and local levels, taking into consideration women's and girls' interests and stressing those beyond their traditionally allotted roles.

Priority should be given to meeting those practical needs (possibly addressing women's condition) which can provide the enabling conditions directed to strategic interests (addressing women's position); or to meeting practical needs in such a way that the question of strategic gender issues arises almost spontaneously.[4]

Combining 'women's practical needs' with their 'strategic interests' is important when literacy activities are designed for women. Programmes or projects that provide knowledge or information that is irrelevant to, or far removed from, the reality and interests of the participants are condemned to failure. The drop-out rate will increase, as will the lack of interest and opposition to enrolment in new courses.

Nevertheless, attention should be drawn to the fact that at times contradictions may arise between development strategies and gender-specific needs and interests. In a presentation to the 1989 Symposium on Women and Literacy, Nelly Stromqvist pointed out that in Nicaragua, in spite of the fact that women's issues had strong government support during the literacy campaign, one of the strategic interests brought forward by women participants, their emanicipation, could not be achieved; the country's unstable situation meant that economic and development strategies took priority.

5. **Participation and organization** Projects and programmes with a participatory approach that includes organizational activities for women and girls constitute the fifth factor. Women should not be simply participants; they should play an active role

in the different stages of the project cycle: identification, design, implementation and evaluation.

Projects or programmes using a participatory approach will need more time to implement than those which do not:

A participatory approach to development will require a *process* rather than the traditional, predetermined, detailed and rigid project. It may also require a specific effort to involve women: their lack of time, their shyness, their powerlessness, sometimes summarized as tradition, may exclude them from decision-making and consultation. On the other hand, co-operation with women to solve a community problem may not help to solve that particular problem, but provide women with experience and visibility as problem-solvers and organizers more generally, thereby improving their status in the household and the community.[5]

The YWCA of India uses a participatory approach involving the formation of groups and the participation of local members in identifying programme needs, planning, implementation and evaluation. In the district of Chandigarh, the YWCA has enabled women to set up a Mahila Mandal (women's group); in several other towns they set up youth clubs. These groups are helping women to mobilize resources for the benefit of the community and to meet their own basic needs.

Apart from these five main factors, there are a number of additional factors which need to be taken into account. For example, the need for literacy activities to be carried out in coordination with government or non-governmental organizations already active in the field, especially when these activities are linked to development projects using an

Chadian refugees at the Habila settlement in Sudan

PHOTO: UNHCR/S.ERRINGTON

integrated approach, is an important factor.

Decentralization of educational activities leads to greater efficiency in implementing programmes or projects. The planning and organization must be sufficiently flexible and dynamic to adapt to the practical situations in the areas where projects are to be carried out. Decentralization is even more important when working with women and girls because their situation may vary from one region to another due to cultural, linguistic, religious and other practices.

Teaching material must be adapted to the particular gender situation and reflect the target group's concerns and interests. Material should not cover too many subjects and topics; this may hinder the teaching/learning process. Teaching methods should be innovative and appropriate; a 'childish' approach that relegates participants to the position of schoolchildren must be avoided.[6]

It is important that contents and methods be flexible and easily adaptable to participants' learning pace, given the women's wide range of tasks at home or in the field which often prevent their regular attendance in courses that follow a rigid pattern.

THE **TIME FACTOR** □ Women are overburdened with work inside and outside the home. Results of a study made by the Women's Programme of the International Council for Adult Education concluded that the daily activities of women in Africa, Latin America and Asia began on average between 4 and 6 am and ended between 10 and 11 pm.

The daily occupations of women vary depending upon their particular country, and whether they live in urban or rural areas, as well as upon climate, ethnic group, tradition and culture. Lack of time in general is a barrier for all women who

The following daily schedule of rural women in Mali serves as an example of how women's time is spent:

4.30 am	Rise.
4.30-6 am	Fetch water; prepare breakfast; attend to children.
6-10 am	Wash dishes; pound millet; collect vegetables or leaves for the mid-day meal; wash clothes; visit market.
10 am-3 pm	Carry the meal to the field; farm on her plot of land, or help the man to till the fields, hoe, weed, plant or guide the plough.
3-6 pm	Gather wood to cook evening meal; collect wild fruit or karité almonds.
6-8 pm	Fetch water; pound millet; clean the compound; prepare the evening meal.
8-9 pm	Card and spin cotton.[7]

wish to follow a literacy course – or any other educational activity – particularly if to do so would mean neglecting their normal routine activities. Other limiting factors, such as time spent caring for children, frequent pregnancies and fatigue are also important. Furthermore, the emigration of men in search of better paid jobs increases substantially women's responsibilities and work, thereby further limiting their chance to acquire literacy.

What can be done to encourage and facilitate women's greater participation and to reduce the rate of their absenteeism and drop-out from literacy activities? Motivation is certainly important, but it is often the day-to-day pressures of work that militate against them taking part. Several NGOs in Latin America and in Asia have organized child-care centres during literacy courses, thus enabling women to attend regularly. In some countries more costly solutions have been considered – such as organizing courses with boarding facilities – which cannot be applied in some regions. A possible alternative is to plan literacy activities by stages, catering for interim periods in which women may undertake individual study at home or elsewhere, rejoining the group at a later stage. This could be especially suitable for rural women who must take part in seasonal agricultural activities.

Whatever option is chosen, the time women have available for study should be discussed and their suggested timetable included in the project's planning stage. It should be generally assumed that literacy activities with women will need more time than with a different target group. One of the findings of a study carried out by G. Carron in South Maragoli in Kenya,[8] where 91 per cent of the participants in literacy courses were women, indicated that their average time to obtain the literacy certificate was 2.4 years whereas normally the average time is calculated to be approximately one year.

LANGUAGE CHOICE □ While many authors have demonstrated the benefits of initial literacy training in the participants' mother tongue, they have also pointed out that the choice should take into account various critera: the language in which participants are motivated to learn and can most easily use in a literate environment; the existence of a written form – and preferably written material – for the language to be used. A linguistic policy also takes into consideration the educational programme in that particular language and, finally, costs and the human resources available.

In a bilingual or multilingual situation, several developing countries have opted for the initial literacy, in the mother tongue, followed by a second, officially accepted, language,[9] for example, largely English in sub-Saharan Africa, French in much of West Africa. The Project for Literacy and Vocational Training for the Native Embera Women in Panama involved both mother tongue and Spanish, supported by bilingual teaching material. By linking this with non-traditional productive activities, the project achieved much better results than would have been possible if only one language had been chosen.

The linguistic options for women and girls who have emigrated to industrialized countries is more clear-cut and involves bilingual courses whenever possible. Several NGOs have organized bilingual literacy courses for women which also provide general information about the host country and the local labour market. For housebound women these organizations offer literacy courses at home, with priority given to teaching the language of the country of immigration.

SELECTION AND TRAINING OF LITERACY PERSONNEL □ If it is agreed that any basic education process intended for girls and women will preferably be implemented by women, particular issues should be considered when selecting literacy personnel. The first of these concerns the cultural aspects of the target group, where the choice of personnel must take into account the particular codes governing relationships among the participants (for instance, those determined by age, ethnic group, caste and religion). The second concerns the definition of the type of engagement, that is to say, voluntary, with incentives or with salary. This is an important element in defining the working situation of these trainers, who will be employed on either an occasional or continuous basis.

Experience has shown that a thorough basic education of female personnel plays a decisive part in the success of literacy activities; it is therefore worth investing in a solid, broadly-based training programme, including continuous retraining. Content cannot be reduced to literacy- and numeracy-teaching techniques; basic knowledge in health, community develop-

ment, group dynamics, civic education, agriculture, applied technology and the production of teaching materials is vital.

A good example is provided by the Experimental Pilot Project in Literacy and Civic Education for Women in Rural Zones, implemented in India in co-operation with UNESCO. Training activities included different courses throughout the year; literacy- and numeracy-teaching techniques were interspersed with several one-week courses organized in such subjects as food conservation, soap-making, production of detergents and silk printing.[10]

ACHIEVING SUCCESS: A SUMMARY OF ESSENTIAL NEEDS □ This educational process is costly, especially when it directly involves the improvement of women's situation in society. The production of written material, the training of women literacy personnel, salaries, transport, motivation and mobilization activi-

ties, and the duration of the literacy process are important elements necessitating adequate financial support. In order to avoid interrupting the educational process, as has happened in many projects that functioned only intermittently, a comprehensive budget should be prepared before the initiation of any programme. Successful programmes and projects must encompass the following:

1. **Political priority and community support**, in order to:
   - Mobilize women
   - Help them complete literacy courses
   - Sensitize groups hostile to women's participation
   - Mobilize the general population
   - Make more resources available
   - Enhance coordination with other activities
   - Help the community to become aware of women's roles and rights

2. **An integrated approach**, in order to:
   - Move easily to meet women's needs

- Help improve women's condition and position in society
- Increase motivation to learn
- Provide useful information in many areas of life

3. **Literacy and post-literacy as a single educational process,** in order to:
   - Foster the creation of a literate environment
   - Support lifelong education
   - Prevent relapse into illiteracy
   - Increase women's chances of continuing formal education

4. **Linkage of literacy to development projects and programmes to meet women's needs,** in order to:
   - Integrate the literacy process into community development
   - Link programmes or projects to local conditions

5. **Providing for women's active participation at every stage of a programme or project; fostering the organization of grass-roots groups for/by women,** in order to:
   - Increase the chance of success and continuity of literacy and development programmes and projects
   - Help in the quest for solutions of shared concerns

6. **Other factors:**
   - Taking into account structural factors such as mobilization, co-ordination and decentralization in order to:
     - increase community support
     - contribute to development
     - increase efficiency of implementation

- Use of teaching methods and contents adapted to women's needs in order to:
  - increase interest in participation
  - facilitate the teaching/learning process

- Considering women's available time for participating in literacy activities so as to:
  - increase their participation
  - decrease drop-out rates

- Choosing the literacy language to facilitate women's integration into the literate community

- Selection and training of women literacy teachers in order to:
  - increase educational efficiency
  - provide a high-quality and effective teaching/learning process

- Taking into account the costs of literacy programmes and projects, and obtaining adequate resources before starting such activities.

1. A Lind, A Johnston, *Adult Literacy in the Third World – A Review of Objectives and Strategies*, Stockholm, Institute of International Education, University of Stockholm/Swedish International Development Agency (SIDA), 1986. (Education Division Documents 32).
2. See P. Freire, *Cartas a Guinea Bissau: apuntes de una experiencia pedagogica* (also in English and French), Madrid, Ed. Siglo 21, 1977; R.H. Dave; A Ouane; D.A. Perera *Learning Strategies for Post-Literacy and Continuing Education: a Cross-National Perspective*, Unesco Institute for Education, Hamburg, 1988; B. Dumont, Post-literacy: a Prerequisite for Literacy, in Literary Lessons, Unesco/IBE 1990.
3. Ibid.
4. K. Young, Introduction: reflection on meeting women's needs, in *Women and Economic Development: Local, Regional and National Planning Strategies.* Oxford/Paris, Berg/Unesco. 1988.
5. Cited in UNDP, *Women in Development: Project Achievement Reports from the United Nations Development Programme*, New York, June 1989, p.46.
6. B. Dumont (1990), 'Post-literacy: A prerequisite for literacy', in *Literacy Lessons*, Geneva, UNESCO/IBE.
7. Malick Sene, 'Un project d'allègement du travail des femmes au Mali' (Summary in English: 'Alleviating Women's Workload in Mali') *Les Carnets de l'enfance/Assignment Children*, Vol. 36. UNICEF Geneva, October-December 1976, pp. 69–70. Reproduced from K. Chlebowska, *Literacy for Rural Women in the Third World*, Unesco, Paris 1990.
8. G. Carron, K. Mwiria, G. Righa. *The Functioning and Effects of the Kenya Literacy Programme: A view from the local level*, Paris, International Institute for Education Planning (IIEP) Research Report 76, 1989.
9. See J.W. Ryan, Linguistic Factors in Adult Literacy, in *Literacy Review*, Teheran, 1980. Also A. Hamadache, D.Martin, *Theory and Practice of Literacy Work: Policies, Strategies and Examples.* Unesco/Canadian Organization for Development through Education (CODE), Paris/Ottawa, 1986.
10. Unesco Principal Regional Office for Asia and the Pacific (PROAP). *Simultaneous Education for Women and Girls: Report of a Project*, Bangkok 1989.

SPREADING THE NET

The introduction to this book noted the limitation of those literacy programmes that focus on strategic development interests when compared with the overwhelming majority of programmes directed towards meeting women's everyday needs.

THIS IS PARTICULARLY TRUE when it is necessary to work within the constraints of poverty and survival. The challenge is to combine literacy efforts concerned with meeting practical gender needs with longer-term strategic interests.

LITERACY AND WOMEN'S RIGHTS □

Some examples of programmes and projects which have taken that challenge into account, at least partially, are described below.

1. **Ecuador: the CEDIME Project** The outstanding aspects of this programme are: consolidation and strengthening of indigenous organizations; preparation of a civic education curriculum incorporating the indigenous culture; discussion of the family role in relation to the local situation; and the establishment of centres for discussion of women's rights on a participatory and non-discriminatory basis.

The different stages of the project included: the development of teaching materials, including a primer on the rights of indigenous women; organization of the participants into women's groups; and innovative methods to strengthen the teaching/learning process.

Materials were developed by CEDIME with the active participation of women and leaders of the Ecuarunari, an indigenous movement. Topics such as health, the family, political participation and organization were selected according to the needs and interests of the participants. The participatory approach included literacy skills, discussion of women's rights and field visits to museums and other communities. The stress given to women's organization and the reinforcement of ethnic and gender identity increased participants' self-confidence and self-esteem.[1]

2. **United States: exercising civil rights** 'I voted today for the first time – and I just can't keep it to myself!' (Margaret, 62 years old). Communities Organized to Improve Life (COIL) is a group of neighbourhood associations, churches and organizations dedicated to improving living conditions in west and south-west Baltimore. One of the organization's most important activities is a literacy programme for 'functional illiterates'. Linking this programme with community development actions resulted in enhanced self-esteem and self-confidence among 'senior citizens'.[2]

3. **The Asia and Pacific Region: women's rights** 'legal literacy' programmes carried out in recent years by the UN's Economic and Social Commission for Asia and the Pacific (ESCAP) in Bangladesh, Indonesia, the Philippines and Sri Lanka are addressed to both literate and illiterate women. The objective is the acquisition of legal knowledge and skills aimed at 'dispelling ignorance (illiteracy) about basic legal rights'.[3]

Within this context the pilot projects try to demystify the law, looking at possible interpretations and applications that may help women exercise their rights, and encouraging legal aid structures and other efforts to mobilize women to use the legal system for improving their quality of life. Women are urged to participate in development and to seek access to power, as well as to analyse and discuss cultural and religious factors which create discriminatory legislation.

There are three levels of action:
1) those encouraging poor, illiterate women in urban, semi-urban and rural areas to participate in literacy, health and income-generating activities;
2) those training professional groups such as women teachers, health workers, journalists and doctors about women's rights, so that they may then, through informal contact, pass their knowledge to women they meet during their professional activities; and
3) those concerned with increasing the general public's awareness of the discriminatory nature of the law.

These programmes thus perform an informative function and may result in legislative changes. They have encouraged participatory studies on the legal status of women, and produced material concerning adverse and discriminatory situations faced by women, often due to negative stereotypes disseminated by the mass media and educational programmes.

4. **Immigrant women in industrialized countries.** The source of many of the problems confronting immigrant women in industrialized countries is isolation: they know neither the language and customs of the host country nor the laws from which they might benefit, or against which they may transgress. Bureaucratic procedures, how to use local transport and how to buy food remain mysteries to these women, who are generally of rural origin. Few have visited towns in their home countries, and they are very dependent on a supportive social net-

work normally provided by the family and neighbours. These interpersonal relationships are an important part of daily life, and provide assistance and information with regard to daily household tasks.

In the host country these women, generally illiterate, find they are isolated from the new environment due to lack of support. Mothers with small children and with little support from their husbands tend to develop an aggressive attitude towards the unknown environment in which they have settled. This attitude is transmitted to their families, increasing misunderstandings with neighbours and authorities, especially because of ignorance of legal and interpersonal relationship codes.

Several NGOs, aware of this problem, have undertaken special programmes for these women to encourage literacy, teach them the language of the host country, address essential administrative procedures of daily life, and/or transmit information about the labour market.

In France, for example, the International Council of Jewish Women (ICJW) is involved in various activities concerned with teaching groups of women to read and write in French. First, participants are initiated into daily life: how to take the metro, to situate the place where they live, to understand administrative procedures and to deal with the authorities and others who can help them to cope better with the new environment. Then, they are introduced to the spoken and written language. Literacy classes bring them together monthly to attend courses over a three-year period, during which social gatherings are organized.

Women attending these courses are better integrated into the community and are better prepared to exercise their

Smaller families mean better health for mothers and children

rights and duties in French society, thereby avoiding misunderstandings which often stem from their marginal situation in the host country.

LITERACY AND HEALTH □ Enabling women to develop literacy can effectively contribute to their own and their families' health and well-being, and by extension to those of their community.

Health education should be geared towards changing those attitudes, values and actions that are discriminatory and detrimental to women's and girls' health. Steps should be taken to change the attitudes and health knowledge and composition of health personnel so that there can be an appropriate understanding of women's health needs. A greater sharing by men and women of family and health-care responsibilities should be encouraged. Women must be involved in the formulation and planning of their health education. This should be available to the entire family, not only through the health-care system but also through all appropriate channels and, in particular, the educational system. To this end, Governments should ensure that information meant for women is relevant to their health priorities and is suitably presented.[4]

Studies in several developing countries have pointed out that women's education plays an important role in reducing infant mortality, increasing the life expectancy of future generations, and improving child rearing and development. It also has a positive impact on reducing birth rates, especially when supported by family planning projects.[5]

More knowledge and understanding of hygiene, child and mother nutrition (especially during pregnancy), control and prevention of diseases (whether these are chronic and/or transmissible), general health practices and child care will enable mothers to improve their own health, as well as that of their infants, their family and the community.

Education is a bridge to understanding how the human body works, which in turn facilitates acceptance of family planning, thus reducing infant mortality (one of the reasons for high birth rates in developing countries) and bringing about a change of attitude favourable to reducing the size of families. Education also enables women and girls to take part, through their own organizations, in community health care and basic health activities, including the use of traditional medicine.

Nevertheless, it must be kept in mind that education programmes aimed solely at changing attitudes will not in themselves help to improve health. Other factors such as poverty and pollution, and even cultural and social patterns, may be harmful to family and community health in general.

Functional illiteracy can have implications for the health of the adult population in industrialized countries too. A Canadian study[6] showed that among the most direct effects were the danger of misusing medicines, mistakes in preparing infant formula, accidents at work and failing to make use of hospital facilities because of the inability to read and write. Indirect effects included ignorance of healthy living habits, of measures to prevent illness during travel, and a tendency towards increased stress due to lack of confidence, depression and anxiety.

The relationship between education and health, and their particular importance for women, has inspired a wide range of literacy activities for women and girls. In most of these literacy programmes teaching methods are oriented towards discussions to raise awareness of problems directly affecting the participants. Many countries, including Bangladesh, Burundi, Cape Verde, El Salvador, India, Indonesia, Mali, Pakistan, Sudan and Thailand include health topics in literacy primers,

PARTICIPE NA LUTA CONTRA A DOENÇA

O Que devemos saber sobre a vacinação das crianças e mulheres grávidas

REPÚBLICA POPULAR DE MOÇAMBIQUE

MINISTÉRIO DA SAÚDE

DIRECÇÃO NACIONAL DE SAÚDE

SECÇÃO DE EDUCAÇÃO SANITÁRIA/SECÇÃO DO PAV

especially those designed for development and child survival programmes;[7] some of them are directed only to women, others to both sexes. Many of these primers cover various aspects of preventive and curative health care, including topics which can stimulate such actions as community sanitation and hygiene, creation of dispensaries and health centres, training of voluntary health workers, and the building and maintenance of wells, latrines, communal garbage dumps and so on.

Another approach adopted by several projects involves the use of posters, booklets, leaflets and other written material to support and motivate literacy and health activities. They focus mainly on post-literacy and community education, as in the case of Kampuchea, where the Programme of the Association of Women, supported, by UNICEF, has produced 25,000 booklets on community health which are currently being used in literacy courses and women's meetings.

The following two examples show how some countries link literacy and health using an integrated and participatory approach, to promote women's family and community health.

1. **Cape Verde** Emigration has long been seen as a means for young people to find new opportunities and escape from poverty. Female heads of household, abandoned by their men, often have several children by various partners who take no responsibility for their paternity, and the women are thus left to carry the whole burden.[8]

Since independence from Portugal in 1975, schooling and literacy programmes have been a governmental priority in Cape Verde. Since 1980 the National Literacy Programme has focused on two priority groups: young people aged 15 to 20 (30 per cent of the country's illiterates) and women of child-bearing age (68 per cent of illiter-

ates). Literacy is not simply confined to the 3Rs, but also includes analysis and discussion of the several subjects contained in the primer: health, sanitary education, the use and maintenance of water, hygiene, traditional medicine, mother/child care, vaccination and immunization, and family planning, as well as history and culture, civic education, agriculture and fishery.

Literacy work is carried out in co-ordination with local health centres. The permanent support received from the Organization of Cape Verdean Women has made it possible to develop an open dialogue with the population in order to attract more women to the health centres. In addition, many such centres now operate as mobile units to provide women with easier access to medical treatment.

2. **Peru** The Asociación Peru-Mujer (Peruvian Women's Association) started a support project for illiterate and semi-literate women in the coastal, mountain and forest regions with the aim of initiating programmes for family planning and immunization in support of family health.[9]

Peru-Mujer developed pictorial materials for participants to colour, about family planning and immunization linked to the living conditions of the participants. These booklets consisted of simple drawings accompanied by paragraphs describing the text and referring to the mode of life and local problems of the family. At meetings the drawings were analysed, discussed in Aymara or Quechua (because the women knew little Spanish) and coloured by the women, or the women took the booklets home where their husbands frequently participated in the colouring process.

The activities carried out at home made it easier for joint discussions with husbands to solve family planning problems. As one women explained, 'the pleasant task of colouring and the ability to identify closely with the family in the booklet made it easier to talk about embarrassing topics like anatomy and contraceptive use'.[10] As a result of this activity, family planning services increased in several areas.

Group discussions helped women to face the problems they shared; several groups set up community pharmacies, called community attention to the need to improve child health services, and involved local authorities in building health centres near their towns.

The positive impact of the project was also due to close co-operation between this national NGO and other organizations working in the same field, such as the Instituto Peruano de Paternidad Responsable (INPARES), the International Planned Parenthood Federation (IPPF) and the Department of Adult Education of the Peruvian Ministry of Education.

PROTECTING THE ENVIRONMENT: A CHALLENGE FOR GENDER-SPECIFIC LITERACY ☐

A significant aspect of enabling women to become literate is their close relationship to the environment and the reasonace this relationship has with agriculture, health and the judicious use of natural resources.

Women are important environmental educators. Young children first learn to see and understand what is happening around them and begin to feel how they are related to it through contact with their mothers. As they grow older, education at home is fundamentally important in planting ethics and in stimulating change in attitudes. Women can also stimulate changes in behaviour that would lead to marked savings in

food, water and energy consumption. Women's education is, therefore, of fundamental importance to enhance their role and active participation in environmental protection and the conservation of natural resources.[11]

In 1987 the World Commission on Environment and Development, presided over by the Prime Minister of Norway, Gro Harlem Brundtland, defined the relationship between the economic system and the environment and established how an imbalance in one affected the other. At the heart of the problem was the demographic explosion, itself closely tied to poverty.

Many analyses concerning the situation of women tend to concentrate on socio-economic and cultural aspects, including employment problems and the considerable responsibility and physical effort that child and family care entail. Matters relating to the environment are generally dealt with superficially, except for those concerning farming and rural women.

Nevertheless, since the mid-1980s there has been a significant increase in studies[12] and international meetings concerning women and their relationship with such environmental factors as energy, water, population, natural resources and urbanization. For the first time, these factors have been linked to their effects on agriculture, child, family and community health, and the conservation of natural resources.

A consensus has emerged on the importance of education and literacy for women as a contribution to the conservation of natural resources and to environmental protection. Women, as the first to suffer from the effects of environmental deterioration and underdevelopment, are usually the first to demand changes. Their role in the family and society makes them particularly anxious and concerned about the well-being of Planet Earth and of future generations. In this context women have several roles to play: as producers, users, consumers and administrators of water, energy, agricultural products, and housing and natural resources; and as educators of their children, through whom they can transmit knowledge that can encourage rational and far-sighted attitudes towards food, water and energy consumption.[13]

The educational role cannot be confined to women alone: the home, community and school are three basic elements in environmental education for children. The concept should therefore be included in the school curriculum to raise awareness about the beneficial effect of careful environmental management. This approach, recently introduced by the joint UNESCO-UNEP International Environmental Education Programme (IEEP), has resulted in 60 countries introducing environmental information into the school curriculum.

Their other roles emphasize women's responsibility for the protection of the environment and conservation of natural resources. Clearly, the effective performance of all these roles is dependent upon a knowledge of environmental matters and an awareness of existing alternatives, which can be acquired only when women become literate.

AGRICULTURE AND FISHING Women are producers, processors and traders in agricultural and food products. They take part in all stages of the production chain, from hoeing, weeding, fertilizing, harvesting and threshing grains to storing produce and buying and selling in the market. Traditionally, women are also often responsible for looking after livestock. They process such goods as cheese and yoghurt, and are involved in the cultivation and preservation of fish for home consumption or sale.

As direct participants in the agricultural

Children learning to grow vegetables at a centre where working mothers leave their pre-school children. Ecuador.

cycle women must focus their activities on the sustainable increase of productivity, the only means of escaping poverty.[14] Often this can be achieved only by changing agricultural practices and methods of, for example, food processing, sale of products and the transport system. But protecting and conserving the environment while increasing production is difficult if women are unaware of the effects of their agricultural practices and how they relate to family health. Moreover, if they cannot read, women will be unable to make proper use of any innovation proposed in this area. To decide whether or not to use a particular fertilizer, mode of transportation or fumigant depends on knowning about their effects on the environment.[15]

WATER, HYGIENE AND SANITATION In developing countries women are the main carriers of water. They are responsible for obtaining and supplying water for domestic and agricultural purposes, as well as for livestock. A woman may need to spend six or more hours a day collecting and carrying water, and this consumes as much as 12 per cent of her daily energy or, in dry mountainous areas, as much as 25 per cent.[16] This exposes them to certain health risks, especially when they are pregnant.

Women decide when and how water is to be used, and they are usually the most affected when water is scarce. Numerous programmes in developing countries to install wells and pumps, and thereby lessen the burden of carrying water over long distances, have not attained their expected results. The low use-rate of these facilities is due not only to the technology employed but also to the attitudes and education of the potential users – women.[17]

Women's particular responsibility for family health, environmental hygiene and

sanitation means that the possibility of their contact with contaminated water is not only a hazard for their own health but increases the risk of infection for their families. Education in the use, management and maintenance of water resources can help women to protect their families from disease, to improve hygiene and environmental sanitation, and to avoid polluting water sources.

Active and organized participation is an indispensable condition for the success of such measures, particular as women are invariably the source of information as to where water is to be found, its availability and quality, and the social acceptability and safety of the source. Women and girls can make an important contribution to ensuring an adequate water supply by participating in the building and improvement of wells, and should be involved in decisions about the location and design, both of wells and of the sanitary, washing and bathing facilities for humans and animals. Literate women are better prepared to take active decision-making roles in these matters.

ENERGY Wood remains the most widely used energy source in many urban and rural areas in developing countries; other sources include agricultural waste and dung. In obtaining fuel men cut trees, women and children collect branches, shrubs and agricultural waste for home use or sale.

Desertification, deforestation and reduced family support due to emigrating husbands increase the effort and time needed to collect fuel, which in turn has negative effects in terms of women's health and the environment. Several studies have pointed out that this situation can result in a decrease in family nutrition, in so far as women prepare up to 50 per cent less food per day in order to save fuel. Natural fertilizers such as dung and humus are often used as fuel instead of as

fertilizers to enrich the soil, and thus agricultural production is negatively affected.

Recent studies have shown that collecting firewood is by no means a major cause of deforestation; in fact, women prefer to collect fallen branches and deadwood for this purpose, as this entails less time and effort. Increasing lumber harvests, indiscriminate agricultural expansion due to forest fires and over-exploitation of the soil, overgrazing and rapid population growth, are the major causes of the loss of the world's forest and their natural resources. Improved stoves designed for a more rational and economic use of fuel have had little effect, as only a minimal quantity of fuel is saved in comparison with that needed for traditional stoves or open fires. A new approach places such stoves in a broader context of family-fuel planning and cooking efficiency.[18]

As literacy raises women's awareness of the implications of misusing energy sources, educational activities should be linked with alternative proposals for a more considered use of these sources. These can include training for reforestation with indigenous and rapid growth species combined with crop production and improved energy use or the use of different forms, for example solar energy for heating, wind energy to power simple machinery, and so on.

POPULATION AND NATURAL RESOURCES

In many countries accelerated population growth goes hand-in-hand with poverty and environmental deterioration, creating serious population/environmental imbalances which have been aggravated by 'environmental refugees'.[19]

One of the commonest ways of slowing population growth is the widespread use of family planning methods. But traditional attitudes and lack of knowledge – especially in rural and semi-urban areas – are major obstacles to be overcome when such a programme is launched. Family planning should not be considered in isolation. Schools should include sex education and family planning in the curriculum. At the community level, literacy and post-literacy materials, for men as well as women, should incorporate information about the human body and its functions with instructions on planning methods. A broadly-based education programme linked to other community activities, with mass media support, should also be considered.

URBANIZATION AND HOUSING In many parts of the world urbanization means lack of adequate accommodation and basic services, overpopulation, shortage of, or lack of access to, potable water, poor sanita-

tion, and other factors which cause disease, high mortality and morbidity rates, and force people to exist in intolerable conditions. With the rapid spread of urbanization, increasing numbers of women and men in urban areas and outlying districts are denied even minimum living standards. It is largely women and children who suffer most from this deprivation. Not surprisingly, the difficulties inherent in coping with urban life and poverty often lead to violence, prostitution and drug addiction.

Women and girls who spend most of their time at home or in the neighbourhood suffer most from the effects of pollution, lack of sanitary facilities, inadequate housing, and lack of transport and work and education facilities.

LIFE IN THE SLUMS

There are many characteristics common to life in these marginal urban areas

Roots
Most slum and shanty-town dwellers are of rural origin. The majority of migrants are driven to town by poverty and start their urban life in the worst areas.

Youth
The average age of slum inhabitants is very low. Large families are traditional in the countryside, and people continue to have them.

Overcrowding
Population density is the highest in the world. It is common to find a family of 10 members sharing one room.

Women householders
In many slums women – abandoned or divorced – are the only providers for 50% of the households.

Squalor
Overcrowding and lack of drainage and sanitary systems create conditions hazardous to health. Rubbish piles up in the street and is not removed.

No services
In these conditions, the need for water and sanitary disposal services is acute. Most slum households must fetch their water from a standpipe and deposit their waste in open drains. The rate of infection is therefore high; there is a constant risk of epidemic.

Malnutrition
Slum dwellers are dependent for their food entirely on cash. As incomes are very low, children are malnourished.

Premature adulthood
Most mothers earn, and are absent from home. Children fend for themselves, in the care of older ones. Many are abandoned, or leave home, at an early age.

Source: El-Hinnawi, E. (1990) modified after UNICEF *News*, Issue 115 (1983) p.11

Literacy and post-literacy training directed specifically at women motivates their participation in innovative construction projects that may include the design, administration and maintenance of accommodation and sanitary and transportation services, as experienced in the Guarari Community Development Project. This low-cost housing programme in Costa Rica, undertaken by a prominent women's organization (COPAM) and the non-governmental organization (COFINE), is a good example of how to incorporate women as planners and resource managers.[20]

When literacy is linked to topics that impart knowledge and promote discussion on urbanization and its short-comings women are better prepared to demand that the relevant authorities provide information on low-cost and local solutions to their housing and environmental problems.

PARENTAL LITERACY AND CHILDREN'S SCHOOL PERFORMANCE ☐

It is generally agreed that the educational level of parents is reflected in the attitudes and values they transmit to their offspring. As the primary source of knowledge, language, values and social relationships, parents play an important role in the initial and future education of children.

Women spend more time with their children than do men, and it is through them that children receive their first perceptions of the world. Initially, mothers transmit habits, attitudes, values and knowledge. Women continue to play an important role as educators; and the higher the educational level of the mother, the more effectively she is able to transmit the knowledge required for her children to achieve a better quality of life. Mothers who drop out prematurely from the education system, or are functionally illiterate, often have low self-esteem and are forced to perform unrewarding work. Such women perceive their lives as patterns of failure and thus transmit negative messages to their offspring, who consequently are subjected to an economic, social and affective climate that perpetuates conditions of poverty and deprivation.

Given that parental educational background influences children's school achievement, the increased number of female heads of household means that it is vital to ensure that women's educational levels are raised in order to interrupt and put an end to the 'inter-generational illiteracy cycle'. In both industrialized and developing countries it has been observed that improving mothers' educational levels increases their interest in enrolling and supporting their children in school. Children are more likely to complete the school year, and girls to remain in school longer: school achievement increases, in part because mothers are able to help with reading and writing skills and with homework. Mothers with a positive attitude towards education and school are more apt to participate in and support school activities, such as parents' and teachers' associations.

Organizing literacy activities for mothers in connection with the education of children is one of the programmes supported by the Unión Argentina de Mujeres (UMA) in outlying neighbourhoods of Buenos Aires. The project was set up to provide literacy for mothers in support of the school activities of their children. Most of the participants were heads of households and had difficulty coping with and improving their living conditions because of the deprived state of the area.

Given the increasing number of malnourished children, the project started a school canteen under the direction of local mothers, and a child-care centre was created to keep children off the street while their mothers worked. Participating neighbourhood women also took part in literacy courses and were taught how better to fulfill their roles in the canteen and the child-care centre. Teachers set up remedial classes to reduce the high level of school drop-outs and assist children with learning difficulties. Meetings, in which reading and writing activities were promoted, were organized between parents and children, and the history of the neighbourhood was discussed and analysed. This shared learning process strengthened ties between teachers, parents and children, and reinforced the literacy activities.

The problem of the 'inter-generational illiteracy cycle' has also been addressed by the Parent and Children Together Project (PACT) in the United States. Combining parents' and children's literacy activities with promoting or improving skills and participation in school activities, the project has organized an education system which merges vocational training and in-school learning. At specified times of the day parents attend courses in the school where their children attend regular classes. At other specified times, parents and children come together to play, read stories or carry out simple arithmetical operations.

This teaching/learning process through game-playing, where children and parents learn from each other, has helped to support learning skills. Parent's interest in their children's school performance increased, particularly as a result of meeting with teachers to discuss and analyse results of the game-playing activities. Many parents stayed on at school after their classes to support teachers' activities, going home with their children to continue the teaching/learning process there.

'Family literacy' is a way of breaking the 'inter-generational illiteracy cycle': it encourages the development of a supportive atmosphere for teaching and learning both at school and at home; it also improves communication skills and encourages parents to read to their children.

LITERACY AND WORKING WOMEN □

In many societies there is a traditional perception about women's work roles. The patriarchal inheritance has permeated behaviour patterns, the power of the law, political and economic systems, religion, the family and the mass media.

There exists, however, another reality in contradiction to the traditional view: women, despite their social and economic disadvantages, bear the greater part of the burden of ensuring that society continues to function. For example, women in many developing countries produce, process and market 80 per cent of the food and perform most of the unpaid work in rural areas. Moreover, these same women undergo repeated childbirth, which often leads to anaemia, are exposed to diseases carried in contaminated water, and their lives are severely affected by the destruction of the environment.

Two-thirds of the world's illiterate population and one-third of all heads of household are women, yet they carry out two-thirds of the work in the informal sector and manage 70 per cent of all micro-enterprises.[21] They also comprise up to one-third of the paid labour force, but receive lower wages than men for the same type of work.

WOMEN IN EMPLOYMENT The female labour force in developing countries has suffered heavily from economic adjustment policies. A reduction of job opportunites and an increase in sub-contracts performed in small-scale family production units are among the results of the global economic crisis. Women become 'self-employed workers' without security and protection and the benefits often afforded to formally employed workers, such as pre- and post-natal leave and the provision of nurseries. In developing countries these conditions affect the poor-

Women employees at Jamshedpur steel plant, Bihar, India

est section of the population, while in the industrialized countries they apply largely to immigrant women.

The electronics sector has made the greatest use of unskilled and young women in developing countries, but the rapid rate of technological innovation makes it difficult for them to rise above the assembly-line level, at which they are usually grossly exploited. Illiteracy and lack of skills are at the root of this problem. Given the growing need for highly-skilled workers in these industries – indeed some have relocated in industrialized countries such as Ireland and Scotland so as to benefit from such a workforce and proximity to consumer markets – priority should be given to linking literacy and post-literacy activities with knowledge relevant in such diverse fields as science, technology and management which could lead to the integration of women into other stages of the production chain.

Gender stereotypes in vocational training and employment must be eliminated, and women encouraged to undertake non-traditional jobs. Gender-specific literacy should also be supported by including technical training in the education system, and by the willingness of employers both to train women on the job and to establish day-care centres for them – a task in which non-governmental organizations could play an active role.

WOMEN IN THE INFORMAL SECTOR

The wide range of activities that women perform in the informal sector renders definition difficult. Morever, cultural patterns deny that certain productive activities are 'work', making it even more difficult to quantify women's participation. Women themselves do not find it easy to establish the dividing line between domestic and income-generating work. Nevertheless, many women work in the informal

THE LIE OF THE LAND

En WID-NEWS 1:90 -SIDA Stockholm 1990

sector and the figure is increasing.

INSTRAW (the United Nations International Training and Research Institute for the Advancement of Women) has suggested a definition appropriately categorizing women's activities as work.

An activity is considered as work when a person:

– works independently or without family help
– carries out jobs requiring little instruction

A JAMAICAN EXPERIENCE

In planning its training for employment programme, the Jamaica Women's Bureau sought advice from the government's Small Industries Division, which forecast that the demand for furniture and equipment for day-care centres would be great, given the government's interest in child-care. The Women's Bureau thus decided to provide training for women in carpentry and welding so that women could satisfy this growing market.

The first training session involved 48 participants and included eight months of technical and business training, an apprenticeship period and time to develop a co-operative structure. Dur-ing all this time, stipends were paid by the government, funds were raised from the Canadian International Develop-ment Authority and Christian Action for Development in the Caribbean for basic equipment and raw materials, and a government rent-free building was secured.

As the project began operation, a major problem arose out of the initial decision to manufacture day-care furniture and equipment. Demand was not nearly as high as anticipated and the project found it difficult to compete with mass-produced goods imported from developed countries. The furniture designs, while attractive, took considerable time to make and raw materials had risen in price since the inception of the project.

The women have since decided to expand the items manufactured to

include desks, chairs, coffee tables and other products that they thought would be in demand locally. Still, most orders come from government ministries. A wider market is needed, but the women received no marketing training and now need advice on this. Since many of the women had experience as small traders, attempts are being made to build on these skills.

While market research for the product proved inaccurate, what is interesting about this project is that it did prove that non-traditional skills for women would increase employability . . . and, in fact, it did! Members left the group because they found higher paying jobs elsewhere. So, while the products did not sell as expected, women were able to increase their income as a result of the project.

– has an income usually lower than those of the formal sector; and

– has limited work prospects and no security.

Women working in the informal sector in developing countries are generally illiterate, have little schooling and few formally recognized skills. Many are the sole means of family support and combine work with family and child-care responsibilities. They earn less than women workers in the formal sector and have little chance of finding another type of job. They often have no access to property. Self-employment is an alternative for women's survival, but conditions in this form of work are often intolerable and, as already noted, offer no health or employment security.

In the informal sector literacy actions should be practical, preparing women for a sector which is vast and unstable, and upon which family income will depend. Preparing women for better income-earning opportunities means ensuring that they become literate. Educational activity must be linked to establishing small enterprises or undertaking income-generating activities which will be the seed for future enterprises.

Certain precautions should be taken when income-generating activities are included in literacy programmes. Results obtained during the 1980s show that these activities have to be treated as enterprises related to the requirements of mainstream economic production, offering continuity and remuneration to the participants. To avoid becoming involved in poorly-rewarded activities, literacy programmes incorporating an income-generating activity should begin with a study of market needs; they should prepare women in non-traditional sectors and for future entry into the formal sector, rather than be directed towards traditional low-level skills which barely supplement home income and which finally become a type of welfare.

Literacy programmes can be linked to entrepreneurial training such as in management and administration of enterprises, accountancy, appropriate technology and marketing. Access to local raw materials to reduce the cost of producing goods, as well as access to credit and property, must be taken into account. An excellent example of combining literacy and income-generation activities is the programme of the Indonesian Department of Community Education, which includes a loan of US$240 to all new literates (most of them women) to set up their own small enterprises.

As shown in the boxed example on the preceding page, a group of Jamaican women organized a small-enterprise project without having received training in marketing, which jeopardized the initial income-generation aim of the project. Once they received training, however, they were able to find jobs elsewhere and increase their income.

1. UNESCO/OREALC/UNICEF, 1989.
2. M.J. Schelmey, 'It's My Turn' in *Momentum*, USA. April 1988.
3. ESCAP, *Guidelines on Upgrading the Legal Status of Women*, (St/Escap/832) Bangkok 1989.
4. The Nairobi Forward-Looking Strategies for the Advancement of Women, United Nations, 1986.
5. See also P. Smyke, Women and World Development Series, Zed Books, London 1991.
6. See Southam Newspaper Group, Toronto, 1987.
7. UNICEF (E/ICEF/1989/6), Geneva 1989.

8. A. Brito, (1990) 'Literacy and family health in Cape Verde, *People* (IPPF), Vol. 17, No. 2, London..
9. J. Haffey, N. Newton et al. (1990), 'Colouring our lives', People, *op. cit.*, pp. 20-21.
10. Ibid.
11. United Nations Environment Programme (UNEP), 1988, para. 60.
12. See, for example, A. Rodda, Women and World Development series, Zed Books, London, 1991.
13. UNEP, 1988.

14. UN, 1989b.

15. Pedagogical material used by the Department of Vegetable Production, Ministry of Rural Development, Guinea-Bissau, 1983.

16. UN, 1989b.

17. M. Elmerdof, Women as Decision Makers, in *Developing World Water*, Grosvenor Press International, New York, 1990, p. 281.

18. UN Vienna, 1989b.

19. UNEP, 1988b.

20. IUCN, *The World Conservation Union Population and Natural Resource Programme*, Case Studies in Population and Natural Resources. Report of Field Investigations and Workshop Discussions, Switzerland, 1990.

21. UN. *The State of the World's Women 1985*, New York 1985.

WOMEN IN FOCUS

Since the 1970s the most widely used approaches in planning literacy activities have been campaigns, use of the media, and special programmes and projects.

A LOOK AT LITERACY ACTIVITIES ☐ Each of the following approaches differs from the others, and although it will not be possible to describe them in detail there is a vast literature on the subject.[1]

LITERACY CAMPAIGNS These are usually organized nationwide, with a strong social mobilization component, embracing a broad group without distinctions based on sex, ethnic group, geographical area and so on. They are generally limited to the acquisition of the three Rs in a relatively short time. They often make considerable use of:

THE MEDIA The written press can promote literacy by taking part in publicity campaigns about the consequences of illiteracy. It can also publish articles to motivate leaders and organizations to carry out literacy activities, and can even carry out such projects and raise support and funds.[2]

Indeed, periodicals, magazines, radio and television are increasingly used in literacy activities, less so in direct teaching or reading/writing and numeracy than as motivating forces targeted at the general public and/or at literacy instructors. In both industrialized and developing countries the mass media has become a tool for raising awareness of the need for literacy, a means of supporting isolated groups of literacy students, and a catalyst at the community level.[3]

THE POWER OF THE PRESS

When a correspondent for a major Canadian newspaper group, Southam News, was unable to determine the extent of the illiteracy problem in Canada, an important chain of events was set in motion. In 1987, the publisher conducted a national in-home literacy assessment of a representative sample of 2,400 adults, the results of which revealed that about 5 million out of 26 million Canadian adults were unable to cope with the ordinary reading, writing, and numeracy demands of the 1980s.

The major shift in Canadian public opinion which resulted from publishing these findings contributed to a decision on the part of the federal government to establish a national literacy secretariat. Provincial governments increased their support to literacy programmes; NGOs became involved on a larger scale; a significant increase in workplace literacy programmes sponsored by employers occurred; and there was a dramatic increase in the number of learners and volunteer tutors who came forward. The survey also provoked a debate on educational issues and policies: on how and why someone with twelve years of education did not possess adequate literacy skills. The Southam survey demonstrates the power of the media to change public perceptions of problems and influence government action to confront them.

Source: ILY, Year of Opportunity, UNESCO, Paris, May 1990, p. 36.

Radio and television can support and encourage enrolment in literacy courses. They have also been used to train instructors and support participation. In the case of multilingual societies they have been used as a means of familiarizing the population with the language of instruction.[4] There are several examples of the use of radio in support of literacy activities and education in general.

In Honduras, radio programmes have been used to promote and supervise literacy, health and agricultural activities.[5] In Colombia, Acción Cultural Popular (ACPO), Radio Sutatensa, supports activities concerning literacy, family planning, human rights and training for adult educators. In Tanzania radio programmes have been prepared to supplement information and knowledge concerning agriculture and health; intended for participants in literacy courses, these programmes have promoted the organization of radio-listeners' groups.

In the United Kingdom, BBC radio and television programmes support literacy activities by making telephone services available to put eventual instructors and participants in touch with each other. Tapes and teaching materials have been produced to train them. One television series, *On the Move*, was created by the BBC in 1975 to reach adults with reading and writing problems.[6]

An interesting experiment in Peru uses video tapes for literacy activities with peasants, and is being successfully applied with women from marginal areas around Lima who are linked to a non-governmental organization, the Asociacion Gabriela Mistral. The results have demonstrated the effectiveness of video tapes in literacy activities when reading, writing and numeracy are linked to women's concerns. It has enabled them to assert themselves in popular community organizations, such as the people's canteens, and the educational process has continued into post-literacy activities.

LITERACY PROGRAMMES These have a systematic plan of activities, usually within a predetermined period. They often include some degree of social mobilization, and may be aimed at particular target groups such as women.

LITERACY PROJECTS These have more precise objectives which generally correspond to those already set in a broader programme. They concern specific areas based on economic, social, cultural, linguistic or other factors, and are the most commonly used approach to literacy activities for women. To be successful, the planning of literacy and post-literacy programmes and projects has to include the factors outlined in chapter 5, regardless of whether the programmes are intended exclusively for women and literacy or as an 'integrated component' in broader programmes, including the participation of both sexes and with the aim of integrating women in development (WID).

ASSESSING WOMEN'S NEEDS □ Project evaluations usually suggest that success is more likely if women's basic motivations and needs are taken into account. The most usual recommendation is that the participants should be asked directly what their needs are, but this does not always seem the most suitable method. The women may have difficulty in the overall perception of problems which require structural changes, and in distinguishing long-term objectives.

Meetings held by women's groups in Ecuador revealed that in many cases there was not only a general failure to realize what their problems were, but also an inability to define objectives and strategies, especially in the drafting of petitions.

The following steps, devised in order to address this issue, are based on experiences in Ecuador, Italy, Togo and Afghanistan:

On the Guajira Peninsula

PHOTO: ILO

1. General and local information should be collected and analysed BEFORE starting to identify needs; this should include knowledge of legal instruments relating to women, and consultations with community experts and leaders on priority needs of the area, especially concerning women.

2. Using a participatory approach, seminars, formal and informal discussions should be organized and a list of priorities established. Women and community leaders should be interviewed, and their replies ranked.

3. An informal discussion group, including community leaders and future participants, should be formed to finalize the list of priorities, and to set up a decision-making group which will select those needs that can favour women's long-term strategic interest, of which they may not yet be aware.

4. The action programme, clearly aimed at improving the condition and position of women, should be one which includes the seeds of change.

This chapter will deal with the methodological aspects of planning programmes and projects using the participatory approach.[7] It will not deal with the preparation of a project document,[8] since standard forms with guidelines can be obtained from international, bilateral or multilateral organizations approached for support. Annex I contains guidelines for a project model, and for an exercise to verify that the different steps have been followed. Annex II provides a reference list of organizations working within the framework of the WID approach, which can advise readers who wish to conduct literacy programmes or projects for women and girls as an integrated component of other programmes concerned with environmental agricultural and industrial development.

PREPARING A LITERACY PRO-GRAMME □ A programme is to be understood as 'a sequence of operations of projects within a broad scheme for meeting an overall development objective'.[9] Using a participatory approach, there are four main stages in a programme cycle – identification, design, implementation and evaluation.

IDENTIFICATION The first question in planning a programme is: *What do we want, and why?* When this has been asnwered, we must decide, within our organization, where we propose to set up this programme. What are the areas of action, and the objectives, of our organization? What is its structure? What specific objectives does it have for women's education? Are there others aimed at this target group – if so, which?

It is necessary then to study and observe the situation of women in the country or region, and, in particular, in the field of education. To involve the women concerned, set up or enlist the help of a women's group with which to study the existing material on the subject or undertake research for more information. Following are some points that it might be useful to research.[10]

• The political, social, economic and cultural situation of women; legislation which favours or prevents them from taking part in development.

• The educational situation: percentage of school enrolment by sex, drop-out rate, participation of women in secondary and in informal education.

• The illiteracy rate for women by regions, access to formal and non-formal education, educational facilities, location of schools and education centres, transport, school and agricultural cycle, multiple responsibilities of women, socio-cultural constraints and linguistic map.

- Educational content of schoolbooks, training material and communication media in connection with stereotypes of women.

- Expenditures on education and health, educational costs, type of schools.

- Measures to promote literacy and post-literacy, technical and vocational education for women, links with the formal and informal sector of the economy, self-employment to increase women's earning capacities.

- Number of women teachers, their qualifications, training, chances of increasing their numbers and improving their skills, women animators active in literacy and post-literacy activities, skills and possibilities of training.

- Structures or number of personnel producing literacy and post-literacy material, use of the mass media.

- Evaluation of actions that encourage and support women's and girls' participation in education.

- Means of distribution of educational material.

When the study has been completed, and problems and possible solutions have been identified, your organization and the women's group will need to decide with whom future work should be coordinated. Programme participants should now be asked about their needs, interests and concerns so that programme objectives may be defined. These must follow a logical order, moving from long- to short-term objectives. Once this is done, the second stage in programme planning can be considered.

DESIGN This stage concerns strategies to be used in carrying out the programme.

The simplest way is to select a women's educational subject related to a broader development plan. Then decide on strategies for literacy and post-literacy activities addressed to women and girls, including areas of implementation, taking into consideration how much time women can spare, and when they are free to participate in such activities. This will enable a programme structure, and potential projects to improve women's status, to be formulated.

Resources required must be identified. Who will be the members of the project team? What qualifications must they have?" What are the financial requirements? Can other types of support be obtained? This information is needed before the programme can be planned and a proposal drafted.

IMPLEMENTATION How is the programme to be administered? How will it be coordinated with other relevant organizations working in the same area? How can effective channels between the programme team and the women it is trying to reach be set up? One way could be a series of meetings at regular intervals, in order to get continuous feedback on the effectiveness of the programme team's work.

FOLLOW-UP AND EVALUATION This final stage is intended to provide information about the programme's progress and alert the team concerning any changes which need to be made. Evaluation informs the funding organization about the extent to which objectives have been attained, and assesses the impact on the target group. Evaluation also assists in preparing new programmes or projects, by utilizing the experience acquired. It must actively involve the participants, for example:

- **Self-evaluation or follow-up** can be carried out by participating women jointly with the programme team and is especially useful for measuring the extent to which short-term objectives have been achieved.

- **Internal evaluation** is also an exercise involving the programme team and the participants. Its objective is to discover whether short-term objectives and activities are related to those of the supporting institution (i.e. the organization to which the application for assistance was submitted).

- **External evaluation** is performed by individuals not involved with the programme but with expertise in the subject. Preferably, part of the team and representatives of the participating women should also be included in order that any ambiguous points may be clarified.

PLANNING A PROJECT □ A project is 'design or undertaking to accomplish specific objectives in response to an identified problem'.[12] The stages in a project cycle are the same as those for a programme: identification, design, implementation and evaluation. But there are differences, especially regarding scale and area of action, as well as the ways in which different activities are implemented.

Experiences in the field of education have shown that small- rather than large-scale projects are usually a more successful option, in that they cover a small area, are more flexible and thus have greater capacity for innovation, are easier to administer and require fewer resources. Small-scale projects make it easier to train a team which will gain experience in the field that can later be applied to a large-scale project, and to assess to effectiveness of the approach selected and the possibilities of extending it to regional or national programmes.

In the case of gender-specific literacy and post-literacy activities, the greatest problem is to find experienced women who can not only produce teaching material but also teach literacy and numeracy skills. A small-scale project is a useful way to train women for later employment of this kind in broader programmes or projects.

IDENTIFYING THE PROJECT First, it is necessary to familiarize ourselves with the community in which we propose to work, visiting the area's streets and neighbourhoods to obtain information about the state of the community's health, housing, agriculture, fishing, commerce and educational buildings and equipment.

This makes possible contact with existing institutions and ongoing projects as well as with community leaders and/or professionals such as nurses, doctors, school teachers and so on. Field visits also allow home visits and informal meetings to explain to the community why we are there and to obtain additional information.

As with programmes, it is important to involve women actively, preferably through a women's volunteer group with which to collaborate in all the future stages of the project. A start can be made with the joint gathering of information required to begin the project: a simple survey can be organized through interviews and observation, talking with community leaders and studying existing documentation.[13] Examples of the type of information that may be needed are given in the chart opposite.

Results of the study can be discussed in community women's groups in order to produce a list of problems, needs and solutions, and ways of coordinating with other community organizations. They should then be presented to community leaders and local women in order to discuss the latter's basic needs and raise awareness with regard to their priorities and their wish to improve their status. Formal and informal discussion meetings can be organized by community women's

General Information:	Number of people: male – female Geographic characteristics of area Climate Electricity supply Central water supply Roads
Economy:	Government and political organization Principal industries – ownership? Number of men and women migrated to area, out of area in last two years. Why? Most common types of employment. How many people earn living in agriculture? What types of crops?
Income:	Control over saleable products Average family income Percentage of net income earned by women Economic arrangements between men and women within household Income-producing activities in the informal sector, i.e. sale of home-made products in local markets, etc.
Education:	Number of schools, vocational and technical courses and centres. Adult education – how many programmes and who participates? Number of boys and girls in schools, to what age
Health:	Most common health problems Number of clinics, maternal child-care centres Number of doctors, nurses or paramedics attending the community
Housing:	Material used in home construction Average number of rooms, and number of inhabitants More than one family in a house? How many own home?
Life and Customs:	Ethnic, religious and linguistic data Daily schedule of a man? Woman? Household/family structures, decision-making and division of labour Means of communication Holidays, cultural centres/activities
Organizations:	Women's groups/organizations Community organizations working on development (government and NGO)
	Source: *ECLA 82*, p.77.

groups in order to determine the project objectives. If the aim is to prepare a literacy and income-generating project the following questions must be asked:

- Does the project use the women's skills? Local materials?

- Is there a market for the products of the project?

- Does it promote self-sufficiency?

- Does it provide women with sufficient training in administration, management and marketing?

DESIGNING THE PROJECT Designing the project strategy includes identification of such resources as personnel, material resources and finance, and may also include a project plan containing definitions about the types of activities to develop (how? when? where?), time available for these activities and the type of financial resources available. The project draft completed on the basis of this information must be discussed with future participants and their amendments incorporated. Guidelines for creating a project model are presented in Annex I.

IMPLEMENTING THE PROJECT means putting the project's aims and objectives into practice by: 1) selecting the project team members and assigning functions and tasks; 2) choosing a coordinator; 3) defining the qualities needed for women's instructors; and 4) selecting the field team.

Defining how the project will operate must be done with the project team. This includes deciding upon project structures and means of co-ordination, both within the project and with other projects or organizations working in the same area. Procedures for meetings of staff, and with the project participants, to decide how and when the proposed activities can be carried out, should also be considered, taking into account the participants' availability.

FOLLOW-UP AND EVALUATION This exercise helps determine problems and needs, can suggest possible solutions, and measures the results and changes achieved following project implementation.

Participatory follow-up and evaluation should always include both the project team and the participants, who can play an active role by proposing new ideas and supporting changes in project implementation. This is crucial when it is necessary to alter the allocation of resources, modify working methods, or decide to retain old, or give new, orientations to the project. Participants can attend formal and informal meetings or seminars to analyse project activities, or take part in an evaluation group. Within this framework, the project should include self-evaluation and self-follow-up and both internal and external evaluations, in the same way as for programmes.

1. See H.S. Bohla. *World Trends and Issues in Adult Education*, Kingsley/UNESCO/IBE, London, Paris, 1989.
2. UNESCO, 1990: *International Literacy Year (ILY)*, Paris, Unesco, 1989. See also UNESCO, *The Role of Media and Fucntional Literacy in Development*, Addis Ababa, April 1983.
3. Ibid.
4. Ibid.
5. R. White, *Mass Communication and the Popular Promotion Strategy for Rural Development in Honduras*. Jamison et al. (eds.) *Radio for Education and Development: Case Studies*, Washington, May 1977.
6. See 2 above.
7. The following have been used as a basis for preparing this content: ECLA *Women and Development: Guidelines for Programme and Project Planning*, Santiago, 1982; ILO, *Proceso Metodologico de Incorporación de la Mujer a la Actividad Productiva*, El Salvador 1988; and C. Overhold et al (eds.) *Gender Role in Development Projects*, USA, Kumarian Press, 1985.
8. Chlebowska, K., 1987, *The Cheli Beli Story*.
9. ECLA, *Women and Development ...*, p.8
10. Based on the document *Women in Development Guidelines by Sector*, UNDP, New York, June 1989.
11. For development of curricula and content to train literacy personnel, see handbooks in English and French produced by UNESCO's Principal Regional Office for Asia and the Pacific (PROAP).
12. See Women's Tribune Center, *Mobilizing Women: How, What, Why and Who of a Project*, New York, November 1981.
13. ECLA 82, p.77.

8 PRODUCING WRITTEN MATERIAL

There is a consensus among adult educators that adults learn better when education is empowering and liberating. Hence, the essence of adult education methodology is, as H.S. Bhola says, a mixture of social ideology and instructional technology.

ONE OF THE MOST IMPORTANT ASPECTS of literacy and post-literacy projects with a gender-specific dimension is the production of written materials. The main steps to be followed when producing a literacy primer for women and girls are briefly discussed in this section, which points out some basic principles governing adult education methods and gives general information on production methods. For those who wish to study the production of literacy materials in more detail than can be encompassed here, the Bibliography provides a list of publications that include information on the subject.

ADULT EDUCATION METHODS: BASIC PRINCIPLES □ Working with adults involves a few basic principles which, if followed, make it possible to bring a suitable approach to the teaching/learning process.

Adults must be considered as such; they should not be treated as children. A quality relationship should exist between instructors and participants, taking into account their knowledge and life experience. Active methods are the most suitable for adults: 'experiential learning, promoting independent learning, critical thinking, problem-solving and learning how to learn'.[1] It is important to encourage the formation of groups whenever feasible; they facilitate learning through the exchange of experience, and help teach how groups function.

The process must be participatory, allowing participants to be actively involved in the teaching/learning process, and must provide tools to enable learners to examine their own reality in order to better understand and change it.

These principles may undergo certain modifications according to the content involved (technological or literary), the context (formal, informal groups or distance education) and the type of group to whom these activites are addressed (age and sex).

PLANNING AND PREPARING TEACHING MATERIALS □ Depending on available financial resources, it may be necessary to choose between different types of materials for literacy activities, i.e. between primers for both literacy and numeracy, or an exercise book, or other types of support materials. Nevertheless, a manual for the literacy instructor should be considered essential support material during the different teaching and learning activities proposed in the courses. If resources permit, it would be wise to include the use of radio and television to motivate and support literacy activities.

LITERACY AND NUMERACY PRIMERS

As has been said before, literacy is not simply the learning of reading, writing and numeracy. It has a broader scope, including the knowledge needed to cope with everyday life. Subjects related to problems, needs and concerns of the target group should, therefore, be included as part of the teaching/learning process, giving literacy activities an integrated approach. Within this framework, preparing a women's literacy primer entails a series of steps:

1. **Organizing a team and fixing learning objectives**
Before beginning to write material we must ask ourselves what we mean by 'an adult literate woman'. The answer, as seen in the box here, will help us to define the goal we wish to reach.

There is general agreement that literate women in both North and South should be able to:

- read the labels on cans and boxes of food
- read a bus or train schedule
- look up numbers in a telephone directory
- read a contract, a health insurance form, a deed, or a waiver
- read a map
- read medical directions
- help their children with homework
- read the menu in a restaurant
- read road signs
- get a job requiring reading or writing
- read the warning labels on poisons and pesticides
- read a letter from a relative or friend and write a response
- keep their own accounts

SOURCE: *ILY, YEAR OF OPPORTUNITY*, UNESCO, PARIS, MAY 1990.

In this way, learning objectives will be achieved in so far as they are directly related to women's concerns. Hence, we must start with research about the women and the community in which we are to work, so as to select suitable subjects.

The Costa Vina Alta de la Molina Project, organized by CENDIP in Peru, provides a good example with regard to production of a literacy primer as part of a literacy and civic education project for rural women. The project started with collective research by instructors and future participants on a sample of 50 households in the community. The information provided by this survey was the basis for production of a primer prepared during several workshops. The workshops, in which the instructors took an active part in producing the materials, also provided them with the necessary training in literacy methods.

2. **Defining a method** There is a wide range of methods for teaching reading and writing. Choices will depend on linguistic and semantic criteria. In general methods fall into three broad groups, traditionally known as synthetic, analytical and global. Synthetic methods stress learning parts of words and sounds (letters) and include alphabetic, phonetic and syllabic methods. Analytical methods base the teaching/learning process on units containing meaning (words and phrases). In global methods, learning comes about through analysis and synthesis of a word, phrase or sentence. While synthetic methods are still used for adults, today there is a growing tendency to use global methods because they are particularly well-suited for learning to read with comprehension.

The example here is from a literacy primer prepared by CODIMCA-Honduras, using the global method. It includes photographs to stimulate discussion of the situation of local rural women. The primer provides information on health, nutrition, hygiene, community development and project planning and implementation, and looks at ways of organizing women's groups and income-generating activities.

As regards teaching numeracy, too often literacy primers attempt to raise social awareness, encourage development and discuss women's situation while at the same time including a very traditional numeracy section using old-fashioned methods taken from traditional primary education. Childish and superficially adapted to women's situation, they do not take into account

Letrina

5. Escribamos las sílabas:

e	le	Le
u		
i		
a		
o		

6. Escribamos y leamos palabras:

ala	bala	cola
Lilia	bola	abuela

1. Observemos y dialoguemos.

2. Leamos la oración:

La <u>mujer</u> merece mejores condiciones de vida

3. Leamos la palabra

<u>mujer</u>

4. Leamos y escribamos las sílabas

mu me mi mo ma
Mu Me Mi Mo Ma

women's traditional mental calculation skills, and lead therefore to poor results. Such material is difficult not only for the participants but also for the instructor, given that its abstract content has no immediate application to local reality. Dalbera (1990) shows how some rural women usually make calculations, and points to the need to consider their 'own way' when developing a numeracy primer.

The effectiveness of teaching numeracy skills depends upon several considerations: it should be addressed to a relatively homogeneous target group, especially ethnically and culturally; it should include an analysis of the women's skills and experiences in mental arithmetic; and it should use those skills first before introducing other systems.

3. **Subjects and content** The content of the primer should match, and respond to,

women's concerns and the need for an improvement in their status in the community. Subjects such as health, agriculture, fishing, industry, civic rights, environment and others may be of interest to the participants, and should be used as the basis for the teaching and learning process.

4. **Writing the primer** Once the issues described in these first three steps have been decided upon, the process of writing the primer can begin. It is important to determine the lessons and content of each primer, the type of exercises and activities to be presented in each lesson, the designs and type of letters to be used, and the ways of evaluating the knowledge acquired. It is essential to take the following into account:

- Use easy language; avoid technical terms and ensure that the subject follows a logical order and sequence.

DERECHOS DE LA MUJER INDIGENA

EDIME

- Graduate the knowledge, moving from the easiest to the most difficult.
- Integrate reading, writing and numeracy in the same text.
- Maintain a unity throughout the chosen subject, using the same characters facing different situations. This enables women to assimilate more easily.

5. **Evaluating the primer** Before involving a large number of women it is clearly advisable to ascertain the effectiveness of the printed material, and a small group of women may be selected to try it out. The results of this exercise can give ideas for relevant modifications. In evaluating the primer the following points should be taken into account: the relevance of the subjects; linguistic, grammatical and arithmetical aspects; illustrations, designs or photos; exercises and

activities; and format. It is important to examine the sequence and graduation of the contents and the clarity of the instructions and proposed teaching activities.

6. **Reproduction and distribution** After making modifications to the primer it can be reproduced on a large scale and distributed in accordance with the planned activities in the field.

7. **Follow-up and evaluation of the primer's impact** It is now necessary to verify that the material has achieved the proposed objectives, and what progress has been made by our target group, Activities[2] such as the following can help to assess the level of reading and writing achieved:
- Did the group learn to read with comprehension? Find a text with short passages containing known

words and only a few new words. Include easy passages taken from books or magazines, for example instructions on the use of medication or on the use of fertilizers and other matters connected with agriculture and the environment. Include maps and road signs, train and bus timetables, telephone directory entries, etc. Ask the participants to summarize what they have read in their own words, explaining the subject and the message that is intended to be trans-

mitted. Ask them to interpret simple directions given as written instructions.

- Did the group learn to write? Prepare a few exercises to find out whether the group can write fluently. Tell a short story or read a text containing an easy vocabulary and ask the women to write about it. Ask them to answer a few simple questions in writing, to write something about a chosen subject from the primer, or to write a letter to a friend or relative.

CATEGORY	FORMAT
1. Printed book	book booklet photo-novella comics etc.
2. Other printed matter	poster leaflets (flyers) wall newspapers news periodicals and journals flipchart picture story-telling hardboard set cards (flash cards, picture cards).
3. Electronic media	films (8 mm, 16 mm) movies videos slides tapes radio programme and TV programme
4. Games and others	1. ordinary conventional game card games, jigsaw puzzles, "future" games, games of finance board games such as sugoroku snakes and ladders 2. simulation game 3. puppet show, shadow play, fork dance, songs
	Source: Guidebook for Development and Production of Materials for Neo-literates, Tokyo: ACCU 1985, p.

POST-LITERACY MATERIALS ☐ Analysis of research carried out in 22 countries by the Unesco Institute of Education (UIE) in Hamburg makes it possible to distinguish twelve types of teaching strategies for post-literacy materials:

1. Newspapers, wallpapers, posters and magazines for neo-literates
2. Textual materials prepared for post-literacy studies
3. Supplementary reading materials
4. Extension literature produced by development agencies such as health departments, agricultural extension services, and so on
5. Radio, TV, video, films, etc.
6. Correspondence courses
7. Libraries for new readers, mobile exhibitions and museums
8. Out-of-school and award-bearing programmes parallel to the school system, and other non-formal courses of a vocational and general character.
9. Occasional programmes based on special needs and interests
10. Local study and action groups
11. Traditional and folk media
12. Sports, games and physical culture

Within these there is a range of written and audio-visual materials that can be used to support newly literate women in various contexts. This type of material can have different formats, as shown in chart here. Given the breadth of the different categories it is not possible to refer to each format, but the most commonly used until now are those in the first two categories.

PRODUCTION OF POST-LITERACY MATERIALS

While literacy materials must be prepared jointly with the participants in literacy projects, post-literacy aids may be prepared either with the participation of new literates or entirely by a team of literacy trainers and suitable personnel. Between the two extremes there are different degrees of participation by trainers and new literates, for example Peru's Literacy and Civic Education Project involved both parties from the beginning through to the final process of booklet production.

Irrespective of the working methods chosen, written post-literacy materials must continue to focus on the participants and include subjects which meet womne's concerns. They should promote dialogue and discussion, have an easy vocabulary and gradually introduce new knowledge. Well designed and illustrated materials are more attractive to the reader.

Producing post-literacy materials is essentially the same process as for literacy materials: research, creation of a working team which includes experienced trainers and new literates, fixing the learning objectives of the written material, selecting subjects and information sources, designing the content structure and writing the material. As with literacy materials, it is important to consider existing practices and beliefs and to present new ideas in a way that does not produce a negative reaction.

It is a good idea, before beginning the booklet, to make a list of the most important ideas of the content, following a logical sequence, and, having brought together these ideas in a simple text, to end with a conclusion, dialogue or discussion. Again, once the material has been drafted it must be carefully evaluated to ensure that the most important information has been covered and that the material is both comprehensible and attractive to the reader. Layout is important: size of the page, margins, typeface used and headings. Illustrations and photographs must clearly transmit the intended message.[3]

Written materials should be field-tested with the intended target group. Annex 1 presents field-test guidelines used by the author in Cape Verde. Such tests enable

KNOWLEDGE	COMMON PRACTICE AND BELIEFS (popular knowledge)	SKILLS
1. What is diarrhoea?	Different types of diarrhoea according to traditional knowledge: • Diarrheoa with bleeding. • Poisonous diarrheoa. • Diarrhoea with fever. • Diarrhoea due to teething. • Diarrhoea due to weaning. • Diarrhoea due to getting chilled. Causes of diarrhoea: internal and external. It is not recognized as a danger for the child's health.	Explain that diarrhoea is a serious infectious illness which must be treated BEFORE it is green, with blood or accompanied by fever. Explain its causes: • germs passing from faeces to the mouth • lack of clean drinking water.
2. Dehydration caused by diarrhoea can kill the child. Give more water as soon as it is detected.	Dehydration is considered an essential treatment: • 'The baby receives sufficient water through food.' • 'Don't give the baby water, the angels will.' • 'The diarrhoea will not stop if you continue to give water to the baby.' continue to give water to the baby.' • 'Avoid water, it stimulates the diarrhoea and cuts the baby's appetite.' Liquids used: Ayran (diluted yogurt), tea, diluted citric acid in tea or water.	Internalize the notion of dehydration as a DANGEROUS treatment. ENCOURAGE hydration as a treatment. Suggested liquids to prevent dehydration: • Mother's milk, gruels, soups, ORS (Oral Rehydration Salts). • Give liquids whenever the baby vomits or there is diarrheoa. • Teach how to prepare ORS. • Encourage giving liquids.

mistakes to be identified and corrected before publication. Again, the material should be first printed and produced on a small scale and its impact evaluated before going into large-scale production.

The following example is a practical application of this procedure, which was followed in the production of a booklet on diarrhoea, addressed to women and girls living in rural and peri-urban areas of Turkey.[4]

• Title: *Mothers are Continuous Doctors* In the planning phase the target group was defined as neo-literate women, the *muhtar* (administrative official), the *imam* (religious leader), traditional midwives and health workers. The material is intended first to inform these groups in their mother tongue (Turkish), with a second part of the booklet for semi-literate women or those using a different language. It may be used at home, in health or community centres, and in coffee houses.

The objective is to help women and the community prevent infant mortality and malnutrition due to diarrhoea, with information obtained from UNICEF's *Facts for Life*, B. Werner's *Helping health Workers to Learn*, and N. Bazoglu's *An Impressionistic Survey on Knowledge: Attitudes and Practices towards Diarrhoea.*[5] Content structure can be seen in the chart here.

Evaluation and the final stages of production were carried out by a group of young women in Ahatli, a peri-urban area of the town of Antalya.

 QUESTION OF TIME A final element to be considered is the time factor in planning programmes, projects and educational materials. Some of the stages will take longer than others, for example a study of women's situation in a community may take several weeks, while training literacy workers can take months. The production of literacy and post-literacy materials will take much longer – up to two years – before it can be fully used. The formation of a literacy work team with a specialist capable of acting at local or national level may take a decade.[6]

The process may, of course, be accelerated, with predictable results such as inefficiencies and increased costs, but it is important to take as much time as possible to build a solid team and good teaching material. Only in this way can literacy objectives be achieved and participating women provided with the tools they need to improve their status in the community and to play an effective role in the development of their society.

1. H.S. Bhola, op. cit. p. 113.
2. Based on Rivera Pizarro, UNESCO/OREALC, 1988.
3. For suitable drawings, consult materials prepared by International Women's Tribune, *The Password is Action*, New York 1988.
4. This booklet was produced by M. Ballara for the UNICEF Office in Turkey in 1988.

5. UNICEF, Ankara 1987.
6. J.W. Ryan, *Planning for Universal Adult Literacy in the Least Developed Countries, Institutional Political and Organizational Obstacles to Universal Adult Literacy* in International Training Seminar for Educational Planners and Administrators from the Least Developed Countries, Paris, 1985.

ANNEX I

A GUIDE TO EDUCATION AND ACTION

THE FOLLOWING DISCUSSION QUESTIONS, arranged chapter by chapter, will help to clarify the various aspects of literacy teaching for women.

DISCUSSION GUIDE

Chapters 1 – 3

1. The traditional sexual division of labour within the family and society prevents many girls from going to school; consequently, women's illiteracy is increasing. How can the coverage and quality of primary education for girls and young women be increased? What measures must be taken to increase enrolment and reduce drop-out?

2. Sub-Saharan Africa and South-East Asia represent the highest percentage and absolute number of illiterate women, with considerable disparity between urban and rural areas. What type of basic educational activities should be carried out in each sector? With what objectives and content? How are basic learning needs to be identified?

3. What does 'functional illiteracy' mean in the context of industrialized countries? What action does it imply?

4. If no urgent measures are taken it is foreseen that the number of functionally illiterate women in industrialized countries will increase. What steps do you think are necessary to tackle the problem? How could NGOs co-operate in the organization, implementation and financing of programmes and projects for women and girls?

5. Is coordination between NGOs and other organizations possible, in order to take concerted action in the struggle against women's functional illiteracy? How can this be organized?

6. Although a consensus now exists concerning the social and economic benefits to be obtained from gender-specific literacy, women and girls continue to face difficulties in enrolling in educational activities. How would you define them, and what measures should be taken to deal with them? How would you apply these measures in planning a programme or project, and what strategies would you use?

Chapter 4

1. The World Conference on Education for All was an event providing a platform for discussion and reflection on the problems of education and illiteracy. How are basic learning needs defined? Do you think that gender problems were given the priority they deserve? Why?

2. UNESCO's Plan of Action and Framework for Action to Meet Basic Learning Needs propose targets, objectives and strategies to speed up the struggle against illiteracy during this decade. What policies and strategies will organizations need to adopt? How will they be implemented? Discuss an action programme.

3. How can mobilization and motivation of personnel working for gender-specific literacy be intensified? What type of training should be given in order to meet women's basic learning needs?

4. How can community volunteers be mobilized to participate as literacy instructors? What incentives and rewards should be offered?

5. How can bilaterial and multilateral agencies and/or NGOs support the objectives of education for all, and women's and girls' literacy activities? How does this relate to your area of action?

6. What type of co-operation might be provided by national authorities to local, national and international NGOs in promoting basic education for women? Give practical examples.

Chapter 5

1. Do you consider proposals made at various international conferences to improve the situation of women are adequate? How would you supplement them? Which of them would you wish to implement in your region or community, and with what objective?

2. Many factors contribute to the success of efforts made by various countries to seek a solution to women's and girls' illiteracy. What, in your opinion, are the most important? Which factors would you add, and why?

3. It is agreed that a correlation exists between family and community health on the one hand and the educational level of women and girls on the other. Which are the worst affected fields? What effect has the economic crisis had on family health? In addition to literacy training, what other actions should be taken?

Chapter 6

1. The mother, as the primary source in transmitting knowledge, influences the values, attitudes and social relations of her family and, in particular, of the children. Discuss the validity of this statement.

2. Experience has shown that the educational level of mothers influences the

schooling of their children and, especially, their daughters: suggest how the present situation can be improved, and explain what is meant by 'family literacy'.

3. Which factors contribute to the degradation of the environment? How do they affect women and the family? What role do women play in educating children in the conservation of natural resources and protection of the environment?

4. If women's and girls' literacy plays an important role in protecting the environment, explain what their contribution could be as regards agriculture and fishing; water, hygiene and sanitation; fuel; population; urbanization and housing?

5. The decrease in job opportunities for women and girls in the formal sector, and increased labour in the informal sector, stem from various factors. Can you list and discuss them? Explain the effects of the economic crisis.

6. Income-generating projects help women to overcome their state of poverty and increase their earnings, but results have not always matched expectations. In your opinion, what have been the achievements and failures of income-generating programmes? Explain how literacy can help in the creation of small and micro-enterprises.

Chapter 7

1. What, in your opinion, is the approach in literacy and post-literacy activities which is best suited to working with women and girls? Why? Organize a discussion concerning the use of mass media in literacy training.

2. What are the stages to be followed in preparing a women's literacy programme? Explain the steps in a project, and how

these differ from those for a programme?

3. What is meant by 'a participatory approach'? How can women be brought more effectively into the process of planning programmes and projects? Which is the best way of obtaining information concerning women's needs, asking them directly or carrying out a participatory-type survey? Why?

4. If adults learn better when education provides access to power, can you state what the basic principles of adult education are and how they can be put into practice?

5. Literacy and post-literacy activities are a single education process. What type of post-literacy training activities could be organized for women and girls?

6. Group exercise: select a real case giving information about the economic, political, social and cultural situation in a community, with particular reference to women and girls. Plan a women's literacy programme or project following the stages proposed. This exercise can be carried out with two or more groups, followed by comparison and discussion of the different strategies and alternatives.

Chapter 8

1. What are the steps to be followed when producing a literacy primer? Give an example of the content of a primer dealing with one or more of the following subjects: a) health, hygiene and sanitation; b) environment; c) formal and informal employment; d) population and urbanization; e) the status of women.

2. Post-literacy written material may have different formats; using the list provided in this chapter, discuss which are the most suitable for women and girls. List and dis-cuss the steps to follow in the production of post-literacy material.

3. Choose a theme and prepare a booklet following the steps proposed in this chapter. Carry out a 'field test' with the group, analyse the results, and discuss the advantages or disadvantages of this activity. If necessary, suggest modifications.

GUIDELINES FOR CREATING A PROJECT MODEL

(OUTLINE OF PROJECT MODEL produced by the International Labour Organization)

The following set of questions can be used to check that the four main stages in the programme or project cycle (identification, design, implementation and evaluation) have been included:

1. Do the necessary conditions and support exist within our organization to carry out literacy and post-literacy programmes for women?

2. How well do we know the situation of women in the place where we wish to act? And the effects of illiteracy on areas such as health, agriculture, fishing, environment and employment?

3. Is the objective to improve the condition and position of women? Are their needs reflected? What results and impact are to be expected?

4. Have we identified the various sub-programmes or projects? The different components of literacy and post-literacy? The time women have available for participation?

5. Do we have sufficient personnel and instructors to carry out the programme? Is training needed – if so, how, when, where and for how long?

6. Have we planned literacy and post-literacy activities as a single educational pro-

cess? Do we need to produce material? Have we provided for channels of distribution?

7. Are literacy and post-literacy activities linked to other community development projects? To the formal or informal employment sector? Can self-employment be generated?

8. With which organizations should we coordinate? Do we have sufficient political support? Can we count on the support of women in the community? Will they be able to take an active part in the four stages of the programme cycle?

9. Have we made provision for joint follow-up and evaluation activities by the project team and the participants? What are the prospects for continuation?

10. Have we identified the necessary financial and material resources and means of application? Are they sufficient for production, reproduction and distribution of materials?

GUIDE TO SELF-EVALUATION AND FOLLOW-UP

The project team, including instructors and literacy participants, can organize a study visit to observe the performance of literacy groups; the material conditions for the activities should be carefully analysed. Subsequently, the following questions should be asked informally of the instructor:

● How many women were enrolled? How many dropped out in the last month?

● Does every participant have a primer? If not, why not? Do they find the primer difficult? How and in which parts? What level of literacy have they reached?

● What other types of activities does the group perform? Do these involve other

groups or individuals? Are other activities planned for the future? When, and with what resources?

● Has the instructor had sufficient training? If not, when is this planned?

Is is useful to organize an informal discussion with the participants on their achievements in literacy and their concerns and needs. List them, and ask for suggestions. Talk with community leaders and ask their opinion on women's literacy activities.

After visiting a representative number of literacy groups, the team will be able to develop a summary of the findings and list possible solutions. The current situation can be compared with the short-term objectives of the programme or project, listing those being fulfilled and those still facing difficulties. If necessary, changes may be proposed in order to solve questions arising during the study visit. The team's progress report can be used as basic information for the next self-evaluation.

HOW TO CONDUCT A FIELD TEST FOR POST-LITERACY MATERIAL

The following exercise was carried out by a group of instructors participating in a seminar organized by Unesco-Breda and the author. It took place in Cape Verde within the framework of the Fogo Island Project on Literacy and Civic Education for Women.

First stage: before going to the field

1. Form an integrated team of three instructors; include if possible some participants, and an instructor using and distributing material. Help them to select the target area/group.

2. The team should decide whether to work with groups or individuals. If with

individuals, it will be necessary to avoid involving other persons during the exercise; if with groups, these should be homogeneous in reading and writing skills and language of communication.

3. The team should study material produced and divide its tasks: an interviewer, and one or two to take notes.

4. The team should simulate a field-test with colleagues, receiving suggestions from them.

Second stage: in the field

1. The team should make a natural contact with the adults. It is important to avoid making adults feel they are being interrogated, or manipulating the answers. The interviewer should explain clearly to the individual or group the purpose of the exercise.

2. First, drawings should be presented without written material, and the following questions asked: What do you see in this drawing (illustrations or photograph)? What do you understand from it? (The note-takers should not ask questions except to clarify answers.)

3. The interviewer should then ask the adult to read a text. If this includes instructions, someone from the group should explain them. Then the following questions should be asked: Did you understand the theme? Can you give some ideas on the subject? Do you understand all the words in the text? Which do you find the most difficult?

4. The note-takers should note the replies and the interviewer should then explain the content of the material. Avoid giving previous information that can help to clarify the content of the written material, and do not write the answers in front of the adults – this may prevent them answering freely.

5. Testing the layout: two or more alternative pages, with different letters (size and design) and presentation (margins, headings, page size) should be provided, and the interviewer should ask which is the easiest to read and understand, and why.

6. When the test is over the team should thank the participants and explain that their suggestions will be taken into consideration in the final preparation of the material.

Third stage: after the field exercise

The team should examine the different answers and correct the written materials in the light of those comments. If necessary, other field tests should be undertaken with different individuals or groups.

ANNEX II
LIST OF
ORGANIZATIONS

INTERNATIONAL AND INTER-GOVERNMENTAL

Council of Europe, BP 431 R6, 67006 Strasbourg Cedex, France

European Economic Community, rue de la Loi, 1049 Brussels, Belgium

International Research and Training Institute for the Advancement of Women (INSTRAW), Santo Domingo, Dominican Republic

International Fund for Agricultural Development (IFAD), 107 via del Serafico, 00142 Rome, Italy

International Labour Office (ILO), 4 route des Morillons, 1211 Geneva, Switzerland

International Monetary Fund, 700 19th Street NW, Washington DC 20431, USA

OECD Development Centre, 94 rue Chardon-Lagache, 75016 Paris, France

United Nations Centre for Social Development and Humanitarian Affairs (UNOV/CSDHA), Division for the Advancement of Women, Vienna International Centre, PO Box 500, A-1400 Vienna, Austria

United Nations Conference on Trade and Development (UNCTAD), Palais des Nations, 1211 Geneva 10, Switzerland

United Nations Development Programme (UNDP), 1 United Nations Plaza, New York, NY 10017, USA.

United Nations Development Fund for Women (UNIFEM), 304 East 45th Street, 1106 New York, N.Y. 10017, USA

UNESCO, 7, place de Fontenoy, 75700 Paris, France

United Nations High Commissioner for Refugees (UNHCR), Centre William Rapard, 154 rue de Lausanne, 1202 Geneva, Switzerland

United Nations Non-Governmental Liaison Service (NGLS), Palais des Nations, 1211 Geneva, Switzerland; also United Nations, New York, N.Y. 10017, USA

UNICEF, 3 United Nations Plaza, New York, NY 10017 USA, also Palais des Nations 1211 Geneva 10, Switzerland

World Bank, 1818 H Street, NW, Washington DC 20433, also 66 Avenue d'Iena, 75116 Paris, France

World Food Programme, Via delle Terme di Caracalla, 00100 Rome, Italy

World Health Organization, Avenue Appia 20, 1202 Geneva, Switzerland

INTERNATIONAL NGOS

Action Aid, Tapstone Road, Chard Somerset, TA 20 2AB, UK

Associated Country Women of the World, Vincent House, Vincent Square, London SW1P 2NB, UK

Bahai'i International Community, Route des Morillons 15, 1218 Grand Saconnex, Geneva, Switzerland

Caritas Internationalis, Palazzo San Calisto, 00120 Cité du Vatican, Italy

Development Forum of the Swedish Churches, Gotgatan 3 NB, 75222 Uppsala, Sweden

Friends World Committee for Consultation (Quakers), Drayton House, 30 Gordon Street, London WC1H OAX, UK

International Alliance of Women, PO Box 355, Valletta, Malta

International Association of Charities, 38 rue d'Alsace-Lorraine, 1050 Brussels, Belgium

International Association of Universities, 1 rue Miollis, 75732 Paris Cedex 15, France

International Catholic Child Bureau, 65 rue de Lausanne, 1202 Geneva, Switzerland

International Catholic Girls' Society, 37-39 rue de Vermont, CP 22, 1211 Geneva, Switzerland

International Council of Jewish Women, 19 rue Teheran, 75008 Paris, France

International Council of Women, 13 rue Caumartin, 75009 Paris, France

International Federation for Home Economics, 5 avenue de la porte Brancion, 75015 Paris, France

International Federation of University Women, 37 Quai Wilson 1201 Geneva, Switzerland

International Reading Association, 800 Barksdale Road, PO Box 8139, Newark, Delaware 19714-8139, USA

International Union of Family Organizations, 28 Place Saint Georges, 75009 Paris, France

Laubach Literacy International, Box 131, 1320 Jamesville Ave, rue Syracuse NY, USA

OXFAM, 279 Banbury Road, Oxford, OX2 7DZ, UK

Soroptimist International, 19 Crofton Court, Heaton, Bradford BD9 5PG, West Yorkshire, UK

Swiss Biblical Society, 2501 Biel, Switzerland

Third World Information Service (I3N), Monbijoustrasse 31, Berne, Switzerland

Women's International Democratic Federation, Unter den Linden 13, Mittelstr. 53-54, 1080 Berlin, Germany

World Association of Girl Guides and Girl Scouts, World Bureau, Olave Centre, 12c Lyndhurst Road, London NW3 5PQ, UK

World Confederation of Organizations of Teaching Profession, 5 avenue du Moulin, 1110 Morges, Switzerland

World Education, 210 Lincoln Street, Boston, Massachussetts 02111, USA

World Federation of Methodist Women, 777 UN Plaza, New York, NY 10017, USA

World Federation of Teacher's Unions, 21 Wilhelm Wolffstrasse, 111 Berlin, Germany

World Federation of Trade Unions, Vinohradska, 12000 Prague 2, Czechoslovakia

World Movement of Mothers, 56 rue de Passy, 75016 Paris, France

World Union of Catholic Women's Organizations, 20 rue Notre-Dame-des-Champs, 75006 Paris, France

Zonta International, 557 West Radolph Street, Chicago, Ill. 60606-2284, USA

GOVERNMENTAL ORGANIZATIONS

CANADA – Canadian International Development Agency (CIDA), 200 Promenade du Portage Hull, Quebec, Canada K1A 064

DENMARK – Danish International Development Agency (DANIDA), Asiastisk Plats 2, 1448, Copenhagen, Denmark

FINLAND – Finnish International Development Agency (FINNIDA), PO Box 276, 00171 Helsinki, Finland

FRANCE – Centre de recherche d'information pour le developpement (CRID), 49 rue de la Glacière, 75013 Paris, France

INDIA – All-India Women's Conference, Sarojini House, 6 Bhawandas Road, New Delhi, India

NETHERLANDS – Organization for International Development (NOVIB), Amaliastraat 7, 2514 JC, The Hague, Netherlands

NORWAY – Norwegian Agency for Development (NORAD), PO Box 8142, Dep 0033 Oslo 1, Norway.

PERU – Centro de Estudios y promocion del desarrollo, 110 Leon de la Fuente, Lima, 17, Peru

Swedish International Development Agency (SIDA), Birger Jarlsgatan 61, 10525 Stockholm, Sweden

UNITED STATES – Agency for International Development (USAID) 320 21st St. NW, Washington DC 20523, USA

BIBLIOGRAPHY

AGFUND/Peru, Ministry of Education/ UNDP (1989), *Alfabetización con video*. Lima, Ministerio de Educación.

Ahmed, M. and G. Carron (1989) The challenge of basic education for all. *Prospects, Quarterly Review of Education*, Vol. XIX, No. 4, pp. 559-72. Paris, Unesco.

Amatyakul, K. and C.O. Jones (1988) Survey of the implementation of a literacy programme in Thailand. *Prospects, Quarterly Review of Education*, Vol. XVIII, No. 3, pp. 389-94. Paris, Unesco.

Asociación Alianza de mujeres costarricense (n.d.) *Encuentro Centroamericano sobre estrategias innovadoras en el tratamiento de la problematica educativa y sociocultural de la mujer en el medio rural y urbano*. San Jose, Costa Rica.

Bagal-Golkap, L. (1990) *Les Femmes et l'Education de base: problèmes et progrès*. Special study for the World Conference on Education for All, Thailand, 5-9 March 1990, mimeo, Paris, UNESCO.

Bernales, A.H. (1979) Radio for the campesino, in K.A. Dikshit et al. *Rural Radio: Programme Formats*. (Monographs on communication technology and utilization, No.5). Paris, UNESCO.

Bhola, H.S.W. (1988) *World Trends and Issues in Adult Education*. Paris/London, UNESCO/Jessica Kingsley. (International Bureau of Education, Educational Sciences.) (1979) *Curriculum Development for Functional Literacy and Nonformal Education Programs*, Bonn, DSE (German Foundation for International Development).

Breda (1983) *Educafrica: Dossier Combattre l'analphabetisme en Afrique*, No. 9.

Brito, A. (1990) Literacy and family health in Cape Verde. *People*, International Planned Parenthood Federation (IPPF), Vol. 17, No.2. London.

Calledois, F. (1989) Women's Literacy for Development: a brief overview of the situation today. Paper presented at the 8-10 June 1989 Symposium on Women and Literacy: Yesterday, Today and Tomorrow, mimeo. Hasselby Slott.

Carron, G. and K. Mwiria (1990) *The Functioning and Effects of Kenya Literacy Programme* (IIEP Research Report No. 76.) Paris, International Institute for Education Planning.

CEE (1985) *Lire et Ecrire: les itinéraires d'analphabetisme*, mimeo. Bruxelles, group de travail analphabetisme.

Chlebowska, K. (1987) The Cheli Beli Story. – (1989a) *Un temps pour apprendre*. April, unpublished. Paris, UNESCO/UNICEF.

– (1989b) Les femmes rurales africaines et l'alphabetisation, *Les Actes de Lecture*, No.28, pp. 66-9. Paris.

Colombo, D., L. Frey and R. Livraghi (1988) The Response of public authorities in Italy to needs expressed by women, in K. Young (ed.) *Women and Economic Development: Local, Regional and National Planning Strategies*, pp. 74-110. Paris/Oxford, UNESCO/Berg.

Dalbera, C. (1990) Arithmetic in daily life and literacy, in *Literacy Lessons*, Geneva, International Bureau of Education (IBE).

Dandekar, R.N. and P.D. Navathe (1985) *5th World Sanskrit Conference, Varanasi*. New Delhi, Rashtriya Sanskrit Sansthan.

Data Highlights No.6: Female Adult Illiteracy (1989) Washington DC/Vienna, United Nations Division for the Advancement of Women, Centre for Social Development and Humanitarian Affairs.

Dave, R.H. et al (1988) *Learning Strategies for Post-literacy and Continuing Education: a cross-national perspective*, 2nd edition (UIE Studies on post-literacy and continuing education, No.1). Hamburg, Unesco Institute for Education.

Demographic and Health Survey Program (1990) Women's Education: Findings for

Demographic and Health Survey. Paper presented 5-9 March to World Conference on Education for All, Jomtien, Thailand.

Dikshit, K.A. et al (1979) *Rural Radio: Programme Formats*, (Monograph on communication technology and utilization, No.5.) Paris, UNESCO.

Dumont, B. (1990) Post-literacy: a pre-requisite for literacy, in *Literacy Lessons*, Geneva, UNESCO/IBE.

Economic Commission for Latin America and the Caribbean (1982) *Women and Development: Guidelines for Programme and Project Planning*. Santiago, United Nations/ECLA.

Freire, P. (1978) *Pedagogy in Process: the Letters to Guinea-Bissau*. New York, Seabury Press.

Gayfer, M. (1987) Literacy in industrialized Countries: a focus on practice. *Convergence: International Journal of Adult Education*, Vol. XX, Nos. 3-4.

Gerhardt, H.P. (1989) Literacy for what? The plurality of cultural approaches. *Prospects, Quarterly Review of Education*, Vol. XIX, No. 4, pp. 491-504. Paris, Unesco.

Gerhardsson, G. (1980) Work sciences and the engineer. *The Environment in Engineering Education*, pp. 19-47.

Grant, J. and P. Adamson (1990) *The State of the World's Children*, New York, UNICEF.

Haffey, J., N. Newton et al (1990) Colouring our lives, *People*. Vol. 17, No.2, pp. 20-21. London, IPPE.

Hall, B.L. (1989) New perspectives in literacy: the role of non-governmental organizations, *Prospects, Quarterly Review of Education*, Vol. XIX, No.4, pp. 573-78. Paris, Unesco.

Hamadache, A. and D. Martin (1986) *Theory and Practice of Literacy Work: Policies, Strategies and Examples*.

Paris/Ottawa, Unesco/CODE.

Harsch, E. (1990) Literacy: an investment in Africa's ecnomic growth. *Africa Recovery*, Vol. 4, No.1, pp. 4-5. New York, United Nations.

IIED/Earthscan (1989) *Our Common Future: A Reader's Guide. The Brundtland Report*. London.

International Labour Organisation (1987) *Linking Energy with Survival: a Guide to Energy, Environment and Rural Women's Work*. Geneva, ILO.

International Planned Parenthood Federation (1990) *Earthwatch* No.38. London, IPPF.

International Water and Sanitation Centre (1990) *IRC Newsletter*, No. 194. The Hague.

International Women's Tribune Center *The Tribune*, No.18 (1982) No. 31 (1985) and No. 42 (1989). New York, IWTC.

Jabre, B. (1988) Women's Education in Africa. *Digest No. 26*, Paris, UNESCO/ UNICEF Co-operative Programme.

Jamison, D.T. and E.G. McAnany (1978) *Radio for Education and Development*, Beverly Hills, California, Sage Publications.

Journal of the International Alliance of Women (1989) *International Women's News*, Vol. 84, No.3. London. IAW.

Jules, D. (1988) Planning Functional Literacy Programmes in the Caribbean. *Prospects, Quarterly Review of Education*, Vol. XVIII, No.3, pp. 369-78. Paris, Unesco.

Junge, B.J. and D. Tegegne (1985) The effects of liberation from illiteracy on the lives of 31 women: a case study. *Journal of Reading*, Vol. 28, No.7, pp. 606-13. Delaware, IRA.

King, E. (1990) *Educating Girls and Women: Investing in Development*. Washington DC, World Bank.

Kotite, P. (ed.) (1989) *Women's Education Looks Forward: Programmes, Experiences, Strategies*. Paris, UNESCO.

Lind, A. (1985) *Adult Literacy in the Third World: A Literature Review*. Stockholm (Report from the Institue of International Education, University of Stockholm, No.73).
– (1990) A Tool for Empowerment of Women. *Voices Rising*, Vol. 4, No.1, pp. 4-5. Toronto.
Lind, A. and A. Johnston (1986), *Adult Literacy in the Third World: A Review of Objectives and Strategies* (SIDA, Education Division Documents No.32.) Stockholm, Institute of International Education, University of Stockholm/Swedish International Development Agency.

McCall, C. (1987) Women and literacy: the Cuban experience. *Journal of Reading*, Vol. 30, No.4, pp. 318-24. Delaware, IRA.
Molyneux, M. (1985) Mobilization without Emancipation. *Feminist Studies*, London.
Munoz Izquierdo, C. (1985) Factores determinantes y consecuencias educativas de la perseverancia de los adultos en los circulos de alfabetización. *Revista Latinoamericana de Estudios Educativos*, Vol.XV, No.3. Mexico City.
Mutava, D.M. (1988) Forty years of struggle against illiteracy: the Zambian case, *Prospects, Quarterly Review of Education*, Vol. XVIII, No.3, pp. 335-49, Paris, Unesco.

Nascimento, G. (1990) Illiteracy in figures, in *Literacy Lessons*. Geneva, Unesco/IBE.
National Center for Family Literacy (1989) News, Fall/Winter. Louisville.
– (1990) Plus Project Literacy. *Special Report on Family Literacy*. Pittsburg.
NGO/EC (1989) *Gender and Development: Combatting Gender Blindness*. Brussels, NGO/EC Liaison Committee.
Nickese, R.S., A.M. Speicher and P. Buchek (1988) An intergenerational adult literacy project: a family intervention/ prevention model. *Journal of Reading*, Vol.31, No.7, pp. 634-42. Delaware, IRA.

Nunez, P. (ed.) (1990) *Alfabetización y educación cívica: experiencia con mujeres campesinas en Peru*. Santiago, Unesco/OREALC.

Ouane, A. (1989) *Handbook of Learning Stratgeis for Post-literacy and Continuing Education* (UIE Studies No.7). Hamburg, Unesco Institute for Education.
Overholt, C. (1988) *Gender Role in Development Projects*, West Hartford, Conn., Kumarian Press.

Quebec Literacy Working Group (1989) *Alert: The Adult Literacy Educator's Reading Tabloid*, Vol.2, No.2, September.

Ramdas, L. (1989) Women and literacy: a quest for justice. *Prospects, Quarterly Review of Education*, Vol. XIX, No.4, pp. 519-30. Paris, Unesco.
Reyes, J. (1990) *Guia metodologica para la elaboración de materiales de lectura*. Santiago, UNESCO/OREALC.
Rivera Pizarro, J. (1988) *Alfabetización*. Santiago, UNESCO/OREALC.
Rodda, A. (1991) *Women and the Environment* (Women and World Development Series.) London, Zed Books/ UN/NGLS.
Rugumayo, E.C. (1987) *The State of the Environment: Education and Training Implications*. New York, Unesco/UNEP.
Ryan, J.W. (1980) Linguistic Factors in Adult Literacy. *Literacy Review*, pp. 57-87. Teheran, IILAM.
– (1985) Some Key Problems in Adult Literacy, Prospects, *Quarterly Review of Education*, Vol. XV, No.3, pp. 375-81. Paris, Unesco.

Sasaoka, T. (1990) How to prepare materials for neo-literates, in *Literacy Lessons*, Geneva, Unesco/IBE.
Scribner, S. and M. Cole (1981) *The Psychology of Literacy*, Cambridge, Mass., Harvard University Press.
Shrestha, S.M. (1986) Women's Literacy

Programme in Afghanistan, mimeo. (Project AFG/79/002). Paris, UNDP/UNESCO.

Singh, S. (1976) *Learning to Read and Reading to Learn: An Approach to a System of Literacy Instruction*. Teheran, Hulton Educational Publications.

Southam Newspaper Group (1987) Broken Words: Why Five Million Canadians are illiterate, in *The Southam Literacy Report*, Toronto.

Stromqvist, N. (1987) Empowering women through education: Lessons for international co-operation. *Adult Education and Development*, No.28.

– (1990) Women and literacy: promises and constraints. *Media Development*, Journal of the World Association for Christian Communication, Vol. XXXVII, No.1, pp. 10-13. Geneva.

United Nations (1986) *The Nairobi Forward-Looking Strategies for the Advancement of Women*. New York, DPI/DESI.

– (1989a) Elements of an International Development Strategy for the 1990s: View and Recommendations of the Committee for Development Planning. New York (ST/ESA/214).

– (1989b) 1989 World Survey on the Role of Women in Development. New York/Vienna, Centre for Social Development and Humanitarian Affairs.

– (1989c) Economic and Social Council: Programme Development in West and Central Africa Region. (E/ICEF/1989/6). Geneva.

– (1989d) ECOSOC: Programme Development in East Asia and Pakistan Region. (E/ICEF/1989/8). Geneva.

– (1989e) Women in Development: Guidelines by Sector, mimeo. New York.

– (1990) Debt: A Crisis for Development, DPI/1032, New York.

United Nations, 1991a, The World's Women. Trends and Statistics 1970-1990, New York.

– (1991b) Special Session on International Economic Co-operation. Resolutions and decisions adopted by the General Assembly during its Eighteenth Special Session (New York, April 1990). International Economic Co-operation, in particular the Revitalization of Economic Growth and Development of the Developing Countries. Suppl. No.2/91 (A/S.18.15). New York.

UNCTAD (1990) *The Least-developed Countries 1989 Report: Highlights. The Least-developed Countries' Experience in the 1980s*. (TD/B/1248). Geneva.

UNDP (1989a) *Education and Training in the 1990s: Developing Countries, Needs and Strategies*. New York, United Nations Development Programme.

– (1989b) *Women in Development: Project Achievement Reports from the United Nations Development Programme*. New York.

– (1990) *Human Development Report 1990*. New York/Oxford University Press.

UNEP (1988a) *The Public and Environment: The State of the Environment 1988*. Nairobi, United Nations Environment Programme.

– (1988b) *Environmental Perspective to the Year 2000 and Beyond*. Nairobi/New York, UNEP/United Nations.

UNESCO (1983) *Equality and Education Opportunity for Girls and Women* (ED-83/WS/55). Paris.

– (1986) *Workshop of Specialists in Europe on Prevention of Functional Illiteracy and Integration of Youth into the World of Work*. Hamburg, Unesco Institute for Education.

– (1988a) *Education of Immigrants: Annotated Bibliography*. Paris, Unesco.

– (1988b) Encuentro Centroamericano sobre Estrategias Innovadoras en el Tratamiento de la Problematica Educativa y Socio-Cultural de la Mujer en el Medio Rural y Urbano-Marginal, Panama, October 1988. *Algunos ejemplos de acciónes educativas innovadoras dirigidas a mujeres que viven en areas rurales y urbanes marginales en otras regiones del mundo*, mimeo. Paris, UNESCO.

– (1989a) *Adult Education Information Notes No.4*, Paris, UNESCO.

– (1989b) *1990: International Literacy Year.* Paris, UNESCO.

– (1990a) *Compendium of Statistics on Illiteracy, 1990 Edition* (Statistical Reports and Studies, No.31). *Compendium des statistiques relatives a l'analphabetisme, Edition 1990* (Rapports et etudes statistiques, No.31). *Compendio des Estadisticas Relativas al Analfabetismo, Edicion 1990,* (Informes y Estudios Estadisticos, No.31). Paris, UNESCO.

– (1990b) *The Challenge: ILY News*, Paris, UNESCO.

– (1990c) *ILY: A Year of Opportunity.* Paris, UNESCO.

– (1990d) *The Unesco Courier*, July. Paris, UNESCO.

– (1990e) *Third Medium-Term Plan (1990-1995.* Paris, UNESCO.

UNESCO/OREALC/UNICEF (1989) *Taller Sub-regional sobre Programas de Educación Civica y Participacion de la Mujer Rural en la Vida Socio-Economica y Cultural de la Comunidad.* Cochabamba (Bolivia), 2-6 October 1989. Memoria de Taller (primer borrador). Cochabamba.

UNESCO/UNEP (1989) *Connect: Environmental Education Newsletter*, Vol. XIV, No.2, June. Paris, Unesco/UN Environment Programme.

UNICEF (1989) *Facts for Life: a Communication Challenge.* New York, UNICEF.

UNICEF/UNEP (1990) *Children and the Environment: The State of the Environment 1990.* New York/Nairobi.

UNFPA (1989) *State of the World Population Report.* New York, UN Fund for Population Activities. New York.

Vargas Vega,. P. (1982) *Materiales educativos y post-alfabetizacion.* Santiago, OREALC.

Vickers, J. (1991) *Women and the World Economic Crisis* (Women and World Development Series). London, Zed Books/ UN/NGLS.

WCEFA (1990) *World Declaration on Education for All, and Framework for Action to Meet Basic Learning Needs.* New York, United Nations Inter-Agency Commission for World Conference on Education for All, Jomtien, Thailand.

Werner, D. and B. Bower (1982) *Helping Health Workers Learn: A Book of Methods, Aids and Ideas for Instructors at Village Level*, Palo Alto, California, Hesperian Foundation.

White, R. (1977) Mass Communication and the Popular Strategy for Rural Development in Hondruas, in P. Spain, D. Jamison et al (eds.), *Radio for Education and Development: Case Studies.* Vol. II, No. 266, pp. 200-60. (World Bank Staff Working Paper.) Washington, World Bank.

Young, K. (ed.) (1988) *Women and Economic Development: Local, Regional and National Planning Strategies.* Paris/Oxford, UNESCO/Berg.

AUDIO-VISUAL MATERIALS

Video-cassettes

The Conception, Illustration and Production of Functional Literacy, Post-literacy and Civic Education Materials for Women. This demonstration video-cassette has been jointly produced by the Asian Cultural Centre for Unesco (PROAP, Bangkok) and the Unesco Secretariat in Paris. Based on materials collected in Asia and the Pacific, it is primarily addressed to that region and to people concerned with the subject. It highlights the main steps, such as:

- constitution of a multi-disciplinary working team;
- motivation and participation of target groups in identification and prioritization of their basic needs;
- presentation of materials in areas such as health, maternal and child care, skills training, awareness of women's rights, women's participation in family and

society, management of small businesses, marketing;

- reproduction and illustration techniques;
- post-literacy materials as part of lifelong education.

Available from: Unesco, 7 Place de Fontenoy, F-75700 Paris, France.

Women and Literacy: Ten agencies and departments of the United Nations collaborated in the production of this half-hour video showing women's projects in Africa, Asia and North and South America, and illustrating how women's literacy is linked to improvements in health, family planning, economic opportunity and awareness of civil rights. It may be obtained from one of the agencies involved (UNESCO, UNICEF, UNDP, UNIFEM, UNFPA, ILO, WHO, IFAD, Division for the Advancement of Women), or from the Department of Public Information (DPI), United Nations, New York, NY 10017.

Films

The following films present the work of four Third World NGO partners of the Netherlands Organization for International Development Cooperation (NOVIB), and are part of a series called Driving Forces directed by Steve de Winter and produced by NOVIB/BELBO. Each film (50 minutes) is in English/Spanish, and available from: NOVIB Film/TV Department, Amalistraat 7, 2514 JC, The Hague, Netherlands.

Women at Work deals with the Kenyan Green Belt Movement, in which women learn to cultivate, plant and take care of trees and fight against the encroaching desert, as well as taking important steps in the struggle for emanicipation.

Children of Cochabamba deals with the international debt crisis. The Instituto de Educacion para el Desarrollo Rural helps Bolivian farmers and their children to counteract the results of the debt crisis.

★   ★   ★

For the other books in the *Women and World Development Series* and for a wide selection of publications on women's issues in general please write to:

Zed Books Ltd.	Zed Books Ltd
57 Caledonian Road	165 First Avenue
London N1 9BU	Atlantic Highlands
United Kingdom	New Jersey 07716
	USA

The books in the Women and World Development series are available free of charge to developing country organizations from:

United Nations Non-Governmental Liaison Service
Palais des Nations
1211 Geneva
Switzerland

INDEX